SEARCHING
HEART, Testing
MIND

Sketch by Leslie

Kevin & Leslie Kerrigan

Dedication

This book is dedicated to our five sons Sean, Kyle, Ryan, Ian and Colin and their lovely wives Rachel, Elyssa, Loran, Lela and Amy. They continually remind us what it is to be young and in love. Each of them inspire us and challenge us in the way that they show their love of God in service to others.

One generation will commend your works to another; They will tell of your mighty acts. (Psalm 145:4)

Acknowledgments

Searching Heart, Testing Mind has been a labor of love. That is fitting since it is, first and foremost, a love story – albeit on many different levels. There is the obvious romantic love that forms the core of the narrative. At the heart of the story is God's gracious love extended to a young man and woman who seek after Him. Underlying it all is the truth of who God is, for He is love. His divine love is seen to cross chasms of culture and language.

Trying to render a true account of events which occurred in days long past, relying on memory alone, has inherent pitfalls. Facts tend to become muddled or at times forgotten altogether. We appreciate reviews of the early manuscript done by Dr. Wally Swanson of HCJB World Radio and Joyce Stuck Grable of Gospel Missionary Union (GMU) for accuracy of the basic facts of the story. Gene Jordan of Missionary Aviation Fellowship (MAF) also reviewed the manuscript for technical accuracy of aviation details. All of them provided valuable cultural and historical insight based on their combined experience of more than a century of living and serving in Ecuador.

Gene's wife, Lynn, a professional educator and consummate grammarian, pored over the manuscript, identifying with red ink errors of spelling, grammar and punctuation. The returned manuscript had the appearance of a newspaper used to line the floor of one of Ecuador's many illicit cock-fighting arenas.

Authoress Lorrie Orr, former missionary serving in Ecuador with both GMU and HCJB, offered inestimable advice on story telling and writing style. Honestly, we will never again be able to simply read a paragraph without having each and every unnecessary adverb practically jump off the page, literally.

About the Authors

Leslie Williams graduated from Biola University with a BS in nursing. She worked as an intensive care unit nurse at various hospitals in southern California prior to marrying Kevin. The next twenty-five years were primarily spent raising their five sons. She then returned to nursing at the local high school near their home in Summerville, SC.

Kevin Kerrigan received a BS from the University of Notre Dame and an MD from the University of South Florida. He completed his surgical internship at Grady Memorial Hospital in Atlanta, Georgia and surgical residency at Naval Hospital, San Diego.

Upon completion of Kevin's surgical training and military obligation, Kevin and Leslie returned with their family to Ecuador where they served at HCJB's jungle hospital for six years. They then re-located their family of seven half-a-world away in Kenya's Great Rift Valley. There they served for two years at Africa Inland Mission's Kijabe Medical Centre.

In 1993, Kevin returned to active duty in the U. S. Navy Medical Corps. The Kerrigans subsequently led groups of youth, church workers, nurses, medical students, residents and physicians on short term mission trips to Ecuador and Kenya.

In 1997, in recognition of their service in Latin America and Africa, Kevin received the American Medical Association's prestigious Dr. Nathan Davis Award for "outstanding contributions in medicine and public health".

Kevin retired from military duty in October, 2007. The Kerrigans currently serve at mission hospitals around the world under the auspices of World Medical Mission.

Chapter 1
Kevin's Arrival

That's snow!

The realization struck me from somewhere in the periphery of my consciousness. By degrees, my mind roused itself from the stupor induced by the long, monotonous flight that had departed Miami six hours earlier. The sight of white peaks beneath me, gleaming in the light of a full moon, was so foreign and unexpected that I could just as easily have been inspecting the surface of a distant planet.

I looked around the cabin to see if any of my fellow passengers shared my startling discovery but, if so, they gave no indication. Several were asleep. The few who were staring out the windows seemed to be lost in thought. Their dark eyes and coarse, impassive features gave no hint as to what was going on inside their heads.

I suppose it's no big deal to them. Most of them have probably been here before, maybe even live here.

I struggled to maintain my outward calm, feeling a bit foolish. It's not like I had to make any effort to appear out-of-place. As far as I could tell, I was the only passenger on the entire flight who had blonde hair and blue eyes. The last thing in the world I wanted to do was draw more attention to myself. I returned my gaze to the dark landscape below, mesmerized by the glittering peaks surrounding the night lights of Ecuador's capital city.

The drab brown fuselage of the Braniff Airlines 707 shuddered as it touched down on the tarmac of Quito's *Aeropuerto Mariscal* one of the world's highest airports, 9300 feet above sea level.

Stepping out of the plane into the clear, crisp night, I descended the steep steps of the boarding ramp. The chill, dry air that greeted me caught me off guard. It was, after all, early July and Quito was situated only a few miles from the earth's equator. I expected weather similar to the suffocating humidity of Tampa, where I had begun my trip earlier that day. This mistaken assumption would prove to be only the first of many preconceived notions that would be turned upside down in the coming days. I was not disappointed by the unexpected chill, however, and found the brisk temperature exhilarating. The night air was filled with a familiar scent that, at first, I couldn't identify. It evoked childhood memories of being sick in bed and having my mother spread a thick slab of Vick's Vap-o-Rub on my chest. In a flash I realized what it was I smelled – the distinct odor of eucalyptus trees. It was competing with, and nearly overcome by, the pungent smell of jet exhaust.

I followed the crowd through the passport check at immigration and awaited my luggage at the carousel. I wished I had made a little more effort to inform someone of the details of my arrival. What if there was no one to meet me in the throng I could see waiting outside the terminal? If I were left on my own, I wouldn't be able to communicate with these people. It was nearly a decade ago that I endured three years of high school Spanish. Any expectation that it would all come rushing back to me vanished during the flight from Miami. I hadn't been able to understand a word of the overhead announcements that the stewardess made. No one seated around me on the plane spoke in English. I felt conspicuously foreign the entire flight. Now, as I stood on the periphery of the shoving, shouting mob gathered around the conveyer belt, the sense of isolation and gnawing fear returned.

Why in the world did I agree to do this? What was I thinking?

My thoughts escaped to the safety of distant memories.

"Doctor Kerrigan, Doctor Kerrigan, please call extension 2000."

I turned on my heel and headed toward the nurses' station, quickening my stride so as to let any witnesses know, beyond the shadow of a doubt, that I was the doctor being summoned by the overhead paging system. The pace of the response was vital – too slow and you might be ignored entirely; too quick and you appeared overly anxious, even panicked. It was important to exude confidence, demonstrating that you were well-prepared to handle any life-threatening emergency that required quick thinking and bold action. It was true that I'd be the last person called in such an emergency. I was still only a lowly medical student. Fortunately, most of the patients and their family members watching me had no way of knowing that. After all, I was wearing a white jacket, universal symbol of infinite knowledge. With any luck no one would take note that it was a short jacket. Only those in-the-know would realize that the length of a white coat was directly proportional to the medical knowledge and experience level of its wearer. We medical students were only allowed to don sports-coat length white jackets. Interns' and residents' jackets got progressively longer, culminating in the calf-length white coats of the God-like attending physicians. At least by now I had moved up a few notches on the food chain. In just a few weeks I'd be starting my senior year. By this time next year I'd be receiving my MD degree and would become a real doctor.

"Can I use your phone to answer my page?"

I tried to make my voice loud enough to sound confidant, yet polite. The pretty, red-headed ward clerk looked up from the stack of orders and lab requests in front of her, not changing her dour expression. Without uttering a word, she nodded at the phone sitting next to her on the desk. To my way of thinking, she did not appear suitably or, for that matter, even remotely impressed. Feeling somewhat deflated, I dialed the extension.

"College of Medicine, Department of Infectious Disease," announced the pleasant voice on the other end of the line. "How can I help you?"

"This is **Doctor** Kerrigan," I replied, being certain to pronounce the title in a clear and commanding voice, "I'm answering a page for this number."

"Oh yes, Doctor Kerrigan. Doctor Reifsnyder was wondering if you had a moment to join him in his office."

"I'll be there immediately."

I emphasized the last word for effect, glancing down at the ward clerk to see if now, at last, she was more appropriately bedazzled. She continued filling out chits without looking up.

Oh, well, the heck with her.

I had more important things on my mind. I was about to embark on a voyage of discovery. As I arrived in the secretary's office of the Infectious Disease department and waited for Dr. Reifsnyder to finish a telephone conversation, I wondered why he had summoned me. I decided that, no doubt, he wanted to give me a last benediction and wish me *bon voyage*.

"Doctor Reifsnyder will see you now," his secretary said with a smile.

David Reifsnyder was a quiet, studious man. His rosy-cheeked baby face and unassuming manner put others at ease. He never talked about himself. I had heard from one of my classmates that he had been raised in Mexico, the son of Protestant missionaries. The full import of that bit of biographical information was about to make itself felt in a most painful way.

"Doctor Reifsnyder?" I said, tapping on his open office door. He looked up from a neat stack of papers on his desk that he had been studying.

"Kevin, come on in. Thanks for coming. How are all the plans progressing?"

"Fine. I got my PPD put on yesterday," I said, showing him the black ink circle on my left forearm marking the site where the skin test for tuberculosis had been placed. "I'll get it read tomorrow."

"Great. Looks like its negative so far," he said, inspecting the area. "Getting excited?"

"I sure am. This was really the last thing I needed to do. I've already gotten my passport, my tickets and my immunizations. It's still hard for me to believe that in just a couple of weeks I'll be down in the Amazon rain forest. I can't wait!"

"Well, that's wonderful. Listen, the reason I called you down here is that I just got these forms from the hospital in Ecuador. Actually, it's from their U. S. headquarters in Miami. Anyway, there are some things they would like you to sign. Just a formality, really."

"Sure, no problem," I assured him as he slid the stack of papers across his desk.

In bold type across the top of the first page was written:

HCJB – Voice of the Andes
That's a weird name for a hospital.

The next line, in slightly smaller print, really caught my attention and set off some inner alarm.

World Radio Missionary Fellowship, Inc.

My heart pounded as my eyes ran down the rest of the page and on to the next. This was some sort of contract. There was a whole list of statements describing activities and behaviors that were deemed inappropriate – such things as smoking, drinking alcohol, cursing and others. Next to each statement was a little line where I was supposed to initial, documenting my agreement to abide by the rules. The sheet trembled in my hand as I was struck by a sudden realization.

The hospital where I'm going to spend my summer is a **mission** *hospital! How could I have been so blind? Why had I not put two and two together? I assumed that the hospital would be run by the Peace Corps or something. What an idiot.*

"Any problem?" Dave Reifsnyder asked, peering into my face. I fought back the rising tide of panic that was washing over me.

"No, no problem," I answered with as much enthusiasm as I could muster.

I realized I was stuck. It was too late to back out now. To do that, I'd have to admit how stupid I had been. Better to just cut my losses and make the best of it. I began initialing each line.

It's really not that big a deal. I don't smoke and I'm not that big of a drinker. Belting down a few beers on the weekend hardly classifies someone as an alcoholic. It is true that I can curse with the best of them, but I learned long ago how to control when and where to use colorful language – never in polite company nor in front of ladies.

The thing about this new wrinkle that irked me was how blind and trusting I had been; that, and the fact that I'd be spending the next three months of my life with a bunch of legalistic religious fanatics.

I can just picture spending the summer sitting around reading the Bible with a bunch of pinch-faced, humorless religious zealots. Oh boy, what fun.

It wasn't that I had anything against religion, really. I mean, I had been pretty religious as a kid. I was an altar boy for awhile and at one point had even toyed with the idea of becoming a monk.

After all, I reasoned, if there really is a God who demands our obedience, why would anyone not live an exemplary life of prayer and quiet contemplation?

But those thoughts occurred during childhood when things were simple. The world got a whole lot more complicated by the time I went off to college. Things had changed and now I was not all that anxious to put myself in the position of having to explain my chosen lifestyle to a bunch of narrow-minded bigots.

What I do with my life is my own affair. I don't have to justify it to anybody. I mean, who do these people think they are trying to get me to sign their petty little contract?

"There you go," I said as I pushed the signed contract back across the desk. "Anything else?"

"Nope. Just learn all you can and have a great time," Doctor Reifsnyder said as he walked me to the door and shook my hand.

"Thanks. I'm sure I will." The irony was inescapable.

Later that day, and throughout the time I had remaining prior to departure, the full weight of this calamitous news began to make itself felt. I was haunted by visions of being backed into a corner by some hellfire and brimstone preacher thumping me on the head with a large, dense, well-worn Bible. The thought dampened my enthusiasm for the trip considerably.

Oh well, it won't kill me. It's only for three months. As my dad used to say, "I could hang by my thumbs for three months". I mean, how bad could it be?

At last my luggage arrived and I made my way through customs. The *aduana* agents gave no more than a cursory glance in my suitcases. I suppose they were disappointed at my inability to understand Spanish. This made me a very poor prospect from whom to extort a bribe. Relieved to have made it thus far, I politely but firmly refused the insistent offers by an army of baggage porters. Exiting the terminal, I waded into the tightly-packed sea of humanity. Everyone, it seemed, was shouting excitedly but, to me, incomprehensibly. A sudden panic seized me.

Now what? What if nobody shows up to meet me?

I fought back the panic and struggled to maintain a brave face. I knew that a tourist who looked lost was an inviting target for con men. I charged ahead, fighting my way through the jostling, noisy gathering. As I reached the edge of the crowd where it began to thin out, a tall, slender woman with a receding chin and narrow face framed by curly dark hair approached me.

"Are you Kevin?" she asked. Relieved to hear the familiar sound of spoken English, I answered enthusiastically that I was.

"My name is Sara Risser," she continued. "I'm the Director of the Health Care Division for HCJB. *Bienvenido al Ecuador.*"

Sara directed me to a nearby van. We placed my luggage in the back, and then exited the airport parking lot heading south into the city.

16

"Thanks for coming to get me," I said. "I was beginning to wonder what in the world I would do if no one was here."

"Well, if you ever find yourself lost in Quito, you can always hop in a taxi and tell the driver '*Hache ce jota be*' – that's HCJB in Spanish. All the cab drivers know it and will bring you straight to the compound."

I repeated the phrase several times till I got it right, and then asked, "I've been meaning to ask someone, what does 'HCJB' mean?"

Sara gave me a quizzical look. "They're the call letters for a gospel radio station here in Quito."

"Oh," I said, still confused. "So what do they have to do with the hospital I'm going to?"

"It's kind of a long story, but I'll give you the short version. HCJB was started by a man from Chicago named Clarence Jones. He looked everywhere for a place to build a radio station and finally ended up here in Quito, even though people told him it would never work. It turned out to be the best place in the world to broadcast from"- she cast a knowing smile – "a mountain on the equator."

"This was when?" I interrupted. I always like to get things chronologically in order.

"Sometime in the 30's," she replied, "during The Depression. Anyway, the missionaries who lived here saw how poor the people were and wanted to help. So about twenty years ago they built a hospital right across the street from the radio compound. A couple of years later, they built another hospital in Shell."

"Oh yeah, that's another thing I wanted to ask about. Shell doesn't sound like a very Spanish name."

"That's because it's not," she laughed. She was obviously enjoying my wide-eyed ignorance about all this.

"The town started out as an oil exploration camp for Shell Oil. This was in the 20's sometime," she said, anticipating my next question. "Later, when they abandoned it, Nate Saint bought it and... you do know who Nate Saint is, right?"

This was asked in the form of a rhetorical question, as though there were only one obvious answer.

"Well, actually, no." I admitted, feeling a hot flush creeping up my neck to my cheeks and on to my forehead.

She looked at me as though I had just arrived on an extraterrestrial spacecraft rather than a commercial jet.

"What about MAF? Ever heard of that?"

My face remained blank.

"Missionary Aviation Fellowship?" she persisted.

Fortunately, I didn't have time to respond. We pulled up in front of a quaint two story building surrounded by a chain link fence.

"Here we are. This is the GMU guest house."

GMU? MAF? HCJB? This alphabet soup is really beginning to annoy me.

"I hate to do this to you, but we're going to need to get an early start in the morning," Sara began.

"We?"

"Yeah, didn't I tell you? I have meetings with the hospital administrator in Shell, so we'll be traveling together. We'll board a bus here in Quito, and then transfer to another bus about halfway there. The whole trip will take seven or eight hours. We'll need to catch a cab by about six o'clock in order to get to the bus station on the south side of town."

"No problem. I'm a morning person. I'll be ready by 6."

One of the guests at the GMU guesthouse who volunteered to stay awake let me in the gated yard. He met me at the front door and handed me my room key, then quickly excused himself to turn in for the night. I found room number 11 on the second floor and fell into bed. Despite the excitement of what promised to be an adventurous time in an exotic location, I had no trouble drifting off to sleep as soon as I laid my head on the pillow.

The next morning I was awakened by a dreadful racket outside my window prior to the time I had set on my alarm clock. Although the guesthouse was located in an urban neighborhood, that didn't prevent the neighbors from keeping barnyard animals. The approaching dawn signaled the local roosters that the time had come to announce the imminent sunrise. The crowing cocks were soon joined in chorus by the neighborhood dogs. Any hope of further sleep was gone. I got up and got dressed.

Sara's taxi pulled up in front of the guesthouse precisely at six. The taxi driver was soon picking his way through a maze of crooked, narrow streets. It was a thrilling ride. If any traffic laws existed in this country, they were universally ignored. But I soon realized that beneath the apparent chaos, an intricate ballet of sorts was taking place to the accompaniment of discordant taxi horns. Vehicles darted in and out of traffic, around circles and through intersections consistently missing one another by inches. As the sun began peeking over the mountains to the east, we arrived at the south end of town and loaded on a bus heading south.

Sara and I settled into the straight-backed bench seat we shared and began to converse. I learned that Sara was raised in a Mennonite community in rural Pennsylvania. She seemed particularly interested in my

Catholic background. I wasn't anxious to share any details. After all, here she was in a Catholic country trying to seduce the population to some brand or other of Protestantism. I could tell she was trying to establish a connection by making a point of letting me know that she had obtained a Master's Degree in Nursing from Catholic University in Washington, D.C. It didn't help her cause. I remained wary.

Keep your guard up, Kevin. You've made it this far without anyone beating you over the head with a Bible. So far, so good. The only question that remains is, how long can it last?

Chapter 2
Leslie's Memories

"Good morning! You must be Leslie Williams."

The voice was way too cheerful for this early hour. I never have been a morning person by nature, but the situation was made even worse by all the time zones I had just crossed. If I had it figured correctly, it was only 5 AM, California time. Plus, my flight from LAX to Quito was delayed a couple of hours, not arriving until after midnight. Still, I wanted to make a good first impression, so I decided to summon up a positive response. But before I had a chance to speak, the cheery voice continued.

"Joyce has told us all about you. She is so looking forward to seeing you again."

The perky, little brunette got up from the dining room table and met me at the bottom of the stairs. Her handshake was as enthusiastic as her voice.

"I'm Emma Becker," she continued, "and this is my son, Timmy."

Timmy sat at the table running his pancakes around the syrup on his plate with a fork. He looked up at hearing his name and smiled at me.

"My husband, Arlowe, is upstairs with the baby. I guess they both decided to skip breakfast this morning and sleep in. Arlowe's been working on the hydroelectric plant in Makuma for the past couple of years. I guess we'll be flying down together this morning. Joyce was hoping we would be able to meet you here at the guesthouse in Quito so you wouldn't have to get down to the jungle by yourself. I'm so glad it worked out this way. What time did your flight arrive last night? You came from California, didn't you?"

As she kept up the constant stream of conversation, she guided me to an empty chair at the table.

"Sit down, sit down. We have so much to talk about."

Emma's warmth and unfeigned interest in me was beginning to win me over, even at this hour of the morning. Just then, the clock in the hallway struck eight. I looked around to see if there were any other guests coming down to breakfast.

"We're the only ones here," said Emma. "A group already left to go to the market in Otavalo and Barb… did you know Barb Youderian's running the guest house now? Anyway, she just left to buy vegetables. Somebody told me a medical student from Florida arrived last night, but he was already gone when I got up this morning."

I poured myself a big glass of water.

"Would you like some pancakes? There's plenty."

"No thanks." I replied. "I'm not much of a breakfast person."

"So, Joyce tells me that you visited them in Yaapi, before they moved to Makuma."

I nodded as I gulped. "Yes, that's right. It was three years ago," I began.

"Well, you've just got to tell me all about it. What did you think of it? Did you like it there?"

"I loved it. As far as I'm concerned, Yaapi is paradise on earth."

Emma smiled appreciatively, encouraging me to go on.

"I mean, true, there were minor inconveniences like no hot water or indoor shower. And, of course, electricity was limited by the amount of diesel that could be flown in to run the generator. But, for me, all of that only added to the adventure."

"I hear what you're saying, Leslie, but just wait until you have kids," Emma said with a smile. "You'll be happy for less adventure and more conveniences. I can't wait to have an electric washing machine."

I was warming to my subject now, oblivious to Emma's concerns about domestic chores.

"I loved visiting villages with John and Joyce, hiking along muddy trails, crossing rivers in dugout canoes, hearing monkeys and toucans in the trees above us, getting caught in sudden rainstorms – I loved it all. But, most of all, I loved spending time with their family."

"So, you knew John, then?" Emma's voice was now softer, lower.

I nodded my head. I felt a sudden rush of emotion and fought back tears.

"Yes," I said, "I met him while I was in college. In fact, that's how I came to Ecuador in the first place."

A man's voice from upstairs interrupted.

"Emma, we need to pack. Hurry. We're supposed to be at the airport in less than an hour."

"I'll be right there," Emma called to the disembodied voice. Then, turning to me, she said, "Sorry to have to run. Hold that thought, though. I definitely want to hear the rest of this story."

With that, she scooped up Timmy and ran up the stairs, leaving me all alone at the dining room table.

Frankly, I was grateful that she got called away when she did. I didn't want to start crying in front of her. After all, I just met her. But being back here in this place released a flood of emotions and memories. Alone now with my thoughts, I reminisced about my first meeting with John Stuck. It came about through a conversation I had with a boyfriend of mine during my last year in high school...

"Really?" said Dave. "You're interested in missions? You should go spend the summer with my aunt and uncle. They're missionaries with GMU."

"What's GMU?"

"It stands for Gospel Missionary Union. That's the organization they're with in Ecuador."

"Where's Ecuador?"

"It's in South America; between Columbia and Peru."

"Have you ever been there?"

"Yeah, I visited them a couple of summers ago. I loved it!"

"What language do they speak there? Spanish?"

"Most of the people do, but Uncle John works with a group of Indians called the Shuar who have their own language. I learned some of it while I was there."

He paused to let the idea sink in. "So, what do you think? Are you interested?"

"Sounds nice, but to be honest, I've always wanted to go to the Congo or somewhere in Africa. But, thanks anyway."

"Well, don't give up on the idea. Even if Ecuador isn't in Africa, you can still get a taste of what it's like to be a missionary. And it's a lot easier place to get to – and cheaper."

Dave knew me well enough to know I couldn't pass up a good bargain.

"Okay I'll think about it."

But as high school came to an end and college loomed on the horizon, my life got busier. Dave's invitation got shoved to the back of my mind. By my third year in nursing school, however, I decided it was time I take a serious look at the mission field. I called Dave to find out how I could contact his uncle.

"You're in luck," Dave said, "he happens to be here in California right now."

"Are you serious? What a happy coincidence."

"Actually, it's not so happy for him." Dave's voice turned serious. "Uncle John was diagnosed with cancer a few months ago."

"Oh, I'm so sorry."

"He's been here getting treated at City of Hope hospital."

"Is his family here with him?"

"No, Aunt Joyce and the kids stayed in Ecuador. But I know Uncle John would love to meet you."

"No, Dave, I couldn't. Not while he's sick in the hospital."

"Oh, don't worry about that. He's out of the hospital now and recuperating at his parents' house. He won't mind your visiting him at all. You'll see."

"Well, all right, I guess. If you really think it's okay. I would like to meet him."

A few days latter I pulled my brown Pontiac sedan into the driveway of Archie Stuck's house in Garden Grove. Archie's wife, Mary, met me at the door and ushered me inside. I was shocked at my first sight of John Stuck. His shirt hung loosely on his broad but gaunt shoulders. Pale skin covered prominent cheek bones. I recognized that this was a very sick man. But out of sunken sockets, his clear, green eyes twinkled.

"Hello, Leslie, so nice to meet you." His grip was strong but gentle. "Dave tells me you're interested in missions."

I prattled on about how I had first heard about missions as a teenager and felt that maybe God was calling me to the mission field. I also told him how God had helped me get through nursing school so far. When I paused for breath, he interjected:

"What would you think of visiting us in Ecuador this summer?"

"Really? That would be great, but ... I don't know."

He sensed my hesitation and interpreted it correctly.

"I know I look like death-warmed-over," he laughed, "but my doctors assure me I'll be good as new now that they've quit poisoning me."

I knew from my training that patients were given treatments designed to poison and kill the cancer cells faster than they killed the body's normal cells. For me, it was a gruesome thought. I was amazed at how nonchalant John was about the whole thing.

"One thing, though. I'll need to run it by my wife, Joyce, to make sure it's okay; but, if I know her, she'll be all for it."

And she was. I doubt there are many women who would have responded like Joyce, if their husbands called to say, "Honey, since we've been apart I've met a young nursing student that I'd like to have come stay with us for the summer."

By summer, John had returned to health and was back in Ecuador with Joyce. I flew down to join them in the jungle village of Yaapi and, as I had been telling Emma, loved every minute of it Always including me as part of their family John and Joyce and the kids made missionary life so much fun. Their love and compassion for the Shuar people they served were an example to me of a living faith. It strengthened my resolve to continue to pursue a career in missions. It also made me long for a family of my own.

One night, as I sat around with the whole family playing a game of Uno, John's laughter led into a bout of coughing.

"John, are you okay?" Joyce asked in a concerned voice.

"Yes, yes, I'm fine," he assured her as he caught his breath and cleared his throat; "just got something down the wrong pipe."

The game went on. I didn't really think much of it until a couple of nights later when the same thing happened again. I felt a heaviness inside. Earlier, John had casually mentioned to me that one of the places most likely for the tumor to return was the lungs. My heart sank as I realized his cough could indicate the spread of his cancer. Joyce gave no appearance of being concerned and I said nothing to her about it.

"You really ought to get that checked out," I said to John one evening after an episode of hacking.

"Oh, great. You, too? It's not enough having one woman hovering over me, worrying about me?" He winked at Joyce. She returned a weak smile.

"John, I really mean it," I persisted. "I know about these things. I'm a nurse, you know – well, almost, anyway." We all laughed.

"Okay, okay, you win, Nurse Williams. Next week, when we take the kids up to Quito to put them in the dorm, I promise," he held his hand up as though taking the Boy Scouts' oath, "I'll submit this mortal coil to a full inspection."

True to his word, John went for a check-up and a chest x-ray the morning after we arrived in Quito. I spent that morning helping Joyce get the kids settled in the dorm next door to the GMU guesthouse. By noon,

Joyce and I had joined the other guests seated around the dining room table of the guesthouse for lunch. Midway through the meal, John appeared and sat down across from us. Anxious to find out the results of his check-up, I blurted out, "Well, how did it go? What did you find out?"

"It's not so good", was all John said, in a calm, quiet voice as he excused himself from the table.

Joyce, alerted by the tone of John's voice as much as by his words, got up from the table and quietly followed her husband upstairs to their room.

Sorry that I had pried my way into an intensely private moment between husband and wife, I attempted to eat the lunch set before me. When I could wait no longer I excused myself and went upstairs. I found Joyce in the women's bathroom crying. One look at her told me that my fears were realized. Joyce filled in the details.

"There is a tumor the size of an orange..." Her voice trailed off.

"I'm so sorry Joyce..."

John's cancer had spread to his lungs.

Within twenty-four hours the entire Stuck family and I were in the air, flying back to southern California. On the plane John sat beside me for part of the trip. I didn't know what to say. We made small talk until...

"John, I know the Lord can heal you and I'm praying that He will."

"Leslie, I know He is able but I don't know what His will is and I don't want to fight Him. I am His, to do with as He pleases."

We sat in silent contemplation. Meanwhile, Joyce sat in an adjoining seat, chatting with the children. She was amazing. Somehow she was able to maintain her cheerful attitude, never letting her fears control her.

Don, Bob and Ruthie, all pre-teens, seemed oblivious to the drama unfolding around them.

The old clock in the hallway, chiming the half hour, brought me back to the present. How ironic that, three years later, here I was back in Ecuador, sitting at the same table where John had revealed his horrible news. I suddenly felt very foolish for being here.

Why in the world did I accept Joyce's invitation to come back for the summer? What am I looking for? It's not like I need to check out living in the jungle to see if I like it. I've already done that. I'm finished with nursing school. I have a year of experience under my belt. I passed my state boards. This is the time I should be heading to the mission field full time, not going for a summer visit. I promised God that if He helped me get through nursing school, I would serve Him overseas. Does my promise to God mean anything, or is it all just talk? What's holding me back from fulfilling my end of the bargain?

I suspected that the answer to that one was fear— I was scared to death that if I went off to some remote location as a single woman, I'd stay that way the rest of my life.

Wouldn't it be smarter to hold off a little while? Just long enough to find that special someone, get married and then go?

I was roused by a soft voice awakening me from my daydreaming.

"Leslie, time to go to the airport. The taxi's out front."

I turned to see the kind face of Emma Becker. She was studying me.

"Oh, Emma, I'm sorry. I just need to run upstairs and grab my bags."

By the time I got back downstairs, the Beckers were in the taxi waiting for me. I felt bad. It was so nice of them to let me share a flight with them. We would fly non-stop from Quito to Makuma, avoiding the eight-hour overland trip to Shell. At the bottom of the stairs I paused and stole one last glance at the dining room. A bittersweet sadness engulfed me. I felt as though I were standing beneath a jungle waterfall with the uneven rhythm of the chilling cascade slapping my head and shoulders, robbing me of air to breathe. I was surprised at what deep emotions this place was able to stir in my heart. I had no idea how much more true that would become in the days ahead.

Chapter 3
Kevin's Introduction

The bus bounced jauntily over the pock-marked road. We were out of the congested city and into fertile valleys. Our route took us south through the *altiplano*, the high plain stretching between the double row of Andean peaks visible on either side of us. All of the hillsides, no matter how steep, were covered with a patchwork quilt of farm fields sporting various hues of green. Here and there the landscape was dotted with fat, black and white cattle. From the valley, we ascended gradually until we reached the top of the pass. On the left, I saw a sign in English and Spanish announcing the presence of a NASA satellite tracking station. From there we began a long, slow descent through an evergreen forest. At one point, we turned sharply to the left and, there in front of us, stood the majestic snow-covered cone of Cotopaxi. It looked close enough to reach out and touch.

"Jeez", I blurted out in astonishment at the sight. Immediately, I sensed stiffening in Sara's countenance. At once, I realized I had committed a *faux pas*.

Oh great. She probably thinks saying "Jeez" is taking the Lord's name in vain – probably thinks I'm some kind of heathen.

But as quickly as her reaction had come, it disappeared, and she said in a natural tone of voice,

"Amazing what God has made, isn't it?"

I agreed in hopes the incident would be quickly forgotten. I didn't want to give her any excuse to start preaching to me.

Further down in the valley we reached the town of Latacunga, where we had to change buses. Latacunga lay directly in the path of lava flow from Cotopaxi and had been destroyed and rebuilt on the same site more than once.

The ordinary bus we had taken from Quito was luxurious compared to the vehicle we now boarded. This one was painted a variety of bright colors and had multi-colored lights strung across the front. There was a metal rack on top loaded with a mix of trunks, old suitcases and wicker baskets filled with everything from produce to live chickens. Sara and I found a seat together. I had to wedge my knees against the metal back of the bench seat close in front of us. We stood out in both appearance and language from the squat, swarthy occupants all around us. These people were mountain Quechuas whose farms fed Ecuador's city dwellers. Quechuas were the descendents of the Incan Empire. Their advanced civilization was subjugated by Spanish conquistadors almost five hundred years ago. Our fellow passengers wore layers of colorful woolen garments, despite the dry noon-time heat. They seemed unperturbed by the sweat it produced, or the resulting odor. Everyone, man and woman alike, was adorned with fedora hats. I felt very conspicuous, dressed as I was in blue jeans and a polo shirt. But I also realized that even if I had been attired in the local costume, my complexion would have given me away.

I sat in silence, wondering what these poor, dirty people sitting all around me were thinking about me. After all, they were descendents of one of the world's great civilizations. Did they regard me as just another foreigner who had invaded their world? Did they in some way hold me responsible for the sins of the conquistadors?

How could they possibly blame me? I'm of Irish and German descent.

Their stoic expressions gave no hint to their inner thoughts, but the vague feeling of uneasiness would not leave me.

An hour or so south of Latacunga we passed through the larger city of Ambato. At that point the asphalt road gave way to a gravel bed which released clouds of dust behind each vehicle that passed. As we left Ambato behind us, I glanced out the bus window. Along the side of the road ahead of us was a large bundle of leaves, about the size of a refrigerator. My glance turned to an intent stare.

"That bush is moving!"

Sara just laughed. As we passed the phenomenon, I turned to see a tiny Quechua woman fastened to the bundle of leaves by a rope tied across her chest.

"If you pay attention, you'll notice it's always the woman carrying the load," Sara said.

"I take it women's lib hasn't made it this far south yet."

"No, not hardly." We returned to our silent reflections.

After a while, Sara asked, "So, do you know what field of medicine you're interested in?"

"Yep – Pediatrics," I replied with more conviction than was warranted. "I sent off applications to several internship programs before I left the U. S."

After a pause I added, "When I started med school I thought I was interested in surgery, but during my second year, when we rotated through the different clinical specialties, it turned out that surgery was my least favorite rotation. So, I've decided on pediatrics – I like kids."

We had just passed over a bridge high above one of the forks of two turbulent mountain rivers that joined to form the Pastaza River. At this elevation, most of the churning brown water came from melted snow on the surrounding peaks. Not far away to the east it would be greatly augmented by the daily downpour in the tropical rain forest. I asked Sara what it was like in the Amazon rain forest.

"It rains every day in Shell," Sara informed me. "They get over two hundred inches a year. That's more than twice what Seattle gets."

We soon entered the mountain town of Baños. Nestled at the base of snow-capped Tungurahua, the town's name derives from the hot springs bubbling up from beneath this active volcano. Baños was populated by dirty, steep-gabled homes looking like neglected Swiss chalets. The bus slowed as we neared the open market. Street vendors approached, hawking their wares: foot-long bundles of split sugar cane as well as some sort of pastry.

"Ever had an *empanada?*" Sara asked. She reached out the window, speaking Spanish to one of the vendors, and then exchanged three large coins for a small brown paper bag. Inside were three of the pastries.

"Try one," she said, holding open the bag. The half-moon-shaped crust was still warm from the frying grease and covered with a sprinkling of sugar. As I bit into it, I found the inside packed with a spicy meat and vegetable concoction. It was delicious.

"They make them with banana or cheese fillings, too", Sara said as she removed one from the bag for herself, offering the remaining one to me. I gratefully accepted.

Just past Baños we entered a tunnel blasted out of solid rock. Upon emerging from the other end, we were greeted by a spectacular view. Foliage-covered cliffs fell steeply to the Pastaza River canyon a thousand feet below us. Waterfalls could be seen on the wall opposite ours, silently and abruptly ending in misted pools. The dirt and gravel road we had been following from Ambato was now carved out of the sheer precipice on the north side of the canyon. Long stretches of the serpentine route were just wide enough to accommodate our bus. There were occasional turnouts for opposing vehicles to await the passage of whichever vehicle got there first. Intermittently along the edge were rusted and twisted vestiges of what had once passed for safety rails.

"Have they ever lost a vehicle over the side?" I asked.

"Oh, yes, but not too often. A more frequent problem is landslides that close the road altogether, sometimes for days."

As we continued to snake our descent along the Pastaza River, three observations marked the transition: towns and individual homes became scarcer and more humble, the air became warmer and much more humid, and the vegetation changed from alpine to tropical. At several points along the way I could have reached out the window and touched lavender wild orchids dangling in profusion from the steep mountainside. As the late afternoon sun began to sink below the Andes range behind us, the land leveled to rolling foothills. The fragrant odor of wild ginger filled the warm, heavy air.

"We're almost there", announced Sara as we entered the outskirts of the latest in a series of grungy little towns we'd begun to encounter: Rio Verde, Rio Negro, Mera and now Shell.

To the newcomer's eye these towns were indistinguishable. Dilapidated wooden structures crowded the edge of the main road on the way into and out of each town. The center of town expanded into an open plaza that invariably contained a large, drab church whose bare concrete walls supported a splotchy patina of mold. Every available wall in town was covered with garishly painted political advertisements advocating one of Ecuador's many political parties. Each party was identified by a number and a distinctive color of paint.

The town of Shell followed the same general pattern with one very obvious difference. The basic layout as described existed on only one side of the road. The land to the south of the road was occupied almost entirely by an Ecuadorian military base, surrounded by barbed wire. Sara explained that Ecuador and Peru had for many years disputed a large tract of rain forest to the southeast of Shell. From time to time this border dispute would break out in open hostilities and skirmishes. There was more than national honor at stake. There were significant petroleum reserves in the *Oriente*, as this tropical area, east of the Andes, was called.

The bus driver discharged us at the front entrance to the military base in the center of town. It was a short walk along the muddy, main road to the mission compound. The compound was dominated by the long L-shaped hospital that was painted a curious teal green. The long arm of the L was a two-story wooden structure paralleling the road. The short arm, an obvious afterthought, was single-story and of concrete block construction.

Epp Memorial Hospital, Shell, Pastaza, Ecuador

We entered by a cement ramp in the middle of the wooden building on the side away from the road. Immediately we received a hearty greeting from the white-uniformed nurse sitting at the nurses' station.

Sara started the introductions. "Lois, this is Kevin Kerrigan, the new medical student."

"Hi. I'm Lois Price. It's nice to have you with us. How was your trip down on the bus?"

I sensed from Lois' open and jovial manner that she was someone who would appreciate a bit of good-natured teasing.

"Other than having my ear chewed off by Sara it was quite pleasant," I joked.

"She can go on, can't she? Well, you both must be beat and famished. Sara, the Peters are expecting you for dinner. Kevin, you'll be eating across the street with Wally Swanson, one of our doctors, and his family. But first you'll want to get moved into your apartment and cleaned up."

Sara bid farewell, grabbed her bag and headed for the Peters' house next door. Lois called out something in Spanish to an unseen companion down the corridor, and then guided me the short distance across an open, grassy yard to an adjacent building. The two-story wooden building, painted the same bright teal as the hospital, was elevated from the soggy earth on concrete pilings. It looked out of place in these surroundings.

"This house is huge. How did it get here?"

"Ev Fuller, the doctor who started this hospital, had seven kids," Lois explained. "He designed this house himself, but when it was built there was some misunderstanding on the dimensions, so it ended up quite a bit larger than he had intended. Now it's divided up into apartments. John and Mary Doerfer and their two kids live on that side. John is our surgeon. You have the downstairs apartment on this side," she said, indicating the left hand side of the building.

The apartment was clean and comfortable, larger than I needed. The small windows and dark paneling contributed to the dank feel of the place. Having lived in Tampa, I was no stranger to the musty odor. After a shower in the four-legged porcelain tub rigged with a cheap, plastic shower curtain, I made my way back across the main road to the building Lois had indicated was the Swanson house. The shape of the roof gave the home a somewhat Oriental appearance. It was adjoined on two sides by the military base. I was met at the door by a thin young man several years my junior.

"Hi, I'm Jeff," he said. "You must be the new med student. Come on in. We've been expecting you."

Jeff was the second of the five Swanson kids. Tod, the oldest, was off to his first year of college. Those left at home in addition to Jeff were Lori, Lisa and Danny. Just as I was trying to get all of their names straight, Charlotte appeared from the kitchen.

Charlotte Swanson was a dominating personality. A Nebraska farm girl, she was gregarious, intelligent and perceptive. When she engaged someone in conversation, she bore into them, giving them her full attention. She was very interested in what others thought, but by no means shy about expressing her own strongly-held views.

"You are just so welcome here," she said. "We are always so happy to have young medical students come to help. Come in and make yourself at home. Lori, why don't you pour the drinks? Lisa, put the blue napkins around." Turning to me, she continued, "We're just waiting for Wally to get home, then we'll eat."

As if on cue, Doctor Wally Swanson stepped through the front door. His slightly stoop-shouldered posture made him look timid, even dull, but closer inspection revealed intelligent eyes bordered on all sides by wavy brown hair, sideburns and mustache. Before he could say a word, Charlotte began the introductions.

"Wally, dear, this is Kevin Kerrigan, our new medical student. He just now arrived after taking the bus all day from Quito."

Wally offered his hand. "Welcome, it's nice to have you." His voice was gentle to the point of being barely audible. He looked as if he was about to say something else, but never got the chance.

"Wally, why don't you go wash up, and then join us at the table. I'm sure Kevin must be starving by now." Charlotte gave me a wide-eyed, smiling look as if expecting confirmation from me.

"Well, there's no rush. I can wait."

"Oh no, no, no, no." Charlotte instinctively entered her mother hen mode as she scurried around, guiding everyone to their place at the immaculately prepared table.

We were soon joined by Wally who turned to Charlotte and said, "Would you like to say the blessing this evening, my dear."

The kids groaned and rolled their eyes. I soon discovered why. Charlotte needed no further prompting. She launched into a protracted and impassioned prayer, begging God's lovingkindness to be showered on friends, family, acquaintances, patients at the hospital, me and lost souls the world over. On several occasions her voice quavered and she seemed close to tears.

When she finally pronounced "Amen", the kids teased that the food would now need to be re-warmed.

"Mom, I've told you how to pray," said Jeff, 'Good bread, good meat, good God, let's eat'". For this, he received a withering stare which, however, Charlotte found impossible to maintain. Soon she was laughing along with everyone else. I felt right at home being with this warm, happy family.

Chapter 4
Leslie's Return

"Olie!" I shouted, as the little red and white Cessna pulled to a stop at the ramp MAF used at Quito's airport. I was so delighted to see the familiar face of pilot Dave Olsen. It was Olie who had flown me from Shell into Yaapi on my previous trip to Ecuador. I reminded him of that fact as we greeted one another.

"Oh, I remember that day well," Olie assured me, "one of the saddest days in my career as a pilot."

After a brief chat, Olie excused himself from the Beckers and me in order to make preparations for our flight. When he was gone, Emma asked:

"What did Olie mean about it being a sad day when he took you into Yaapi?"

"Well, after he let me off, Olie got a radio message diverting him to Puyupungu to pick up the body of a young man who had drowned."

"Oh, how awful."

"He was one of a group of college kids who had come down to help out for the summer. I had been talking with them the night before."

"So, you knew the young man?"

"No, not really," I admitted. "His name was Jim Buckholtz, but I wasn't even really sure which of the kids he was. The day after we met with them, the whole group took a hike from Shell to Puyupungu. As they were crossing the river, Jim got swept off his feet and washed away. I guess they found him in a whirlpool a short distance downriver."

Emma shuddered as she pulled her infant and toddler closer to herself.

"There's a group of summer helpers in Makuma right now. We call them the Baltimore gang."

"It was really sad," I continued. "I heard that Jim's parents weren't all that crazy about his coming to Ecuador in the first place, so they took it pretty hard. I think he was studying to become a concert pianist or something. Anyway, Olie had to fly his body back to Shell. He's buried somewhere near there."

"Olie is such a sensitive, caring person," Emma observed.

"That's for sure. I remember one time Olie flew Joyce and me into Kusuimi. Just as we were landing, some turkeys began walking across the airstrip. Instead of hitting them, Olie quickly maneuvered over them, knowing how valuable they were to the Indians. Joyce and I were so impressed."

A voice behind me interrupted, "Well, I hate to disillusion you." It was Olie. "But the real reason I avoided those turkeys was for our benefit, not theirs. I had just gotten a letter from a pilot friend of mine in Papua New Guinea. A pig ran across just as my friend was landing and he hit it, breaking his landing gear in the process. As it was, my avoiding those turkeys almost caused us to have an accident. As I recall, I ended up making a forced ground loop. I might have been better off making turkey casserole that day."

We all laughed.

"Alright, enough chit chatting," said Olie. "Let's get you folks down to Makuma while the weather holds."

Olie didn't have to convince us. We were all well aware of how dependent MAF's flight plans were on weather conditions. Heading south from Quito wasn't usually the problem. It was descending through the mountain pass from Baños to Shell that was the most treacherous part of the flight. The pass was so narrow that it seemed to me I could reach out the window and touch either side. And that wasn't the worst. Because of its location where the mountains and the rainforest meet, the pass regularly experienced thick fog and mist that would suddenly appear out of nowhere, obscuring all vision. Even successfully navigating the pass didn't mean you were home free. Frequent torrential downpours throughout the rain forest kept pilots always ready to change their flight plans. On this day, however, it was clear sailing all the way.

Once we left the danger of the Baños pass behind us and headed out over the monotonous rain forest, my mind began to drift back to an incident that had occurred a couple of months before.

Okay, that's the third ring.

It annoyed me when I realized that I was twirling and untwirling the springy cord around my left index finger. I yanked my finger free and began to hang up the receiver.

Oh well, at least I can tell her I tried to call.

Just then a syrupy voice came over the line. "Hello?"

"Oh. Hi, Kathy. You are there. I thought I had missed you."

"Hi, Leslie. No, I'm here alright. I've just got so much to do. Addressing these invitations is taking me a lot longer than I had thought. Plus, I need to get lesson plans ready for the teacher who will be subbing for me this coming week. Then, to top it all off, this morning my car wouldn't start. I don't know how I'm going to get everything done. Did you have a chance to get fitted for your bridesmaid's dress?"

I don't know how she did it. Even when she was complaining about having too much to do, she said it in such a sweet tone that it made you want to comfort and caress her. Most days I found her sweetness very appealing, but not today. Today, it grated on my nerves, especially considering the purpose of my call.

"Yeah, I did go down to the dress shop today, Kath. Actually, that's the reason I called."

She must have caught something in the way I said it, because there was a kind of awkward pause. I decided to plunge on in.

"Kathy, I know I told you I would be a bridesmaid, but I just don't know how I can do it."

"What? Leslie, what are you saying?"

"Look, remember I told you months ago that I was planning to go to Ecuador again this summer ..."

"But that's not until after the wedding," she said.

Her tone was pleading. I could tell she was on the verge of tears, but her voice still sounded so sweet. I wished she would at least get mad or something.

"I know, but the truth of the matter is I just can't afford to do both."

It was the truth. I was trying to save enough money to cover my apartment rent and car payments for the time I would be in Ecuador. But, if I was honest with myself, I'd have to admit that it wasn't the whole truth. Somewhere in the mix of my thoughts and feelings, I had to suppress an ugly argument that kept popping up. Secretly, selfishly I was not all that excited about taking part in another of my girlfriends' weddings. Since last year when we had all graduated from college, practically our whole group had fallen in love and walked down the aisle – with me trailing behind them. There were only a couple of us left unattached. A vivid picture kept painting itself in my mind, even though I tried to erase it. It was the sneer on the face of an old boyfriend of mine as he remarked about a mutual acquaintance, "Well, she's just an old maid..." I felt a knot in my stomach each time I remembered it and realized that the girl he was talking about at the time was two years younger than I was now!

I always presumed that I would some day get married. Attending a Christian university seemed a likely place to meet a life partner who shared my values and beliefs. Where better to meet a man who shared my vision of serving God in some foreign land?

At first, I had resisted the idea of attending a Christian college. After all, I had enjoyed sharing my faith with fellow students at the public high school I attended. Why would I want to go to a school where everyone already knew the Lord? But then a friend pointed out what a unique opportunity I might have at a school like Biola University to influence tomorrow's Christian leaders.

"Tell me," he said, "of the Christian friends you have, how many are excited about their faith, wanting to share it with others?

"Not many" I admitted, "in fact, very few."

"Well then, if the Christians being trained in Christian institutions aren't excited about their faith, how can they encourage others to have a vibrant relationship with God?"

I saw the wisdom in what he said and, shortly after, applied for admission to Biola. As it turned out, I loved it. Much to my surprise, qualities that had caused me to be on the fringe of popularity in high school – such as my habit of asking deep questions of new acquaintances – turned out to be great assets in college. I enjoyed the unaccustomed popularity and attention, especially from the opposite sex. Yet, somehow, at the end of my time at Biola, I had no better prospects for marriage than when I had enrolled five years earlier. It wasn't for lack of desire on my part.

There were a number of young men who had shown interest in me. My natural friendliness and sociability led to lots of opportunities to meet eligible prospects, despite the 3 to 1 ratio of women to men. I reveled in the attentions of a series of interesting and admirable young men. Yet, most of them had no interest in foreign missions and I found that the ones who did held no fascination for me.

So, here I was, about to follow another of my college friends down the aisle with the man of her dreams. It wasn't that I resented my friends for finding husbands, but I was really beginning to wonder.

Will I ever find that special someone?

"But, Leslie, you just have to be in my wedding." The sweet voice on the other end of the line was wavering now, about to crack. I felt terrible.

"Look, Kathy," I tried to sound more conciliatory, "try to understand. I'm going to be in Ecuador for three months. I won't be making any money and I'm still going to have to pay my share of the apartment and keep up car payments. I just don't see how I can do all that and pay for the bridesmaid dress as well."

I remembered my shock when I first saw the price tag of the dress she had chosen. Even Kathy would have to admit that the dresses were a bit extravagant. It was more than I had ever paid for any dress. But Kathy came from money, so it might not have seemed so out of reach to her. As for me, on the other hand – that was a different story. I was on my own as a working girl trying to make ends meet. I had a good job as a nurse in the intensive care unit at Orange County Medical Center. It paid well, but they got their money's worth out of us. Caring for some of the sickest patients in the hospital was very stressful, and not everyone could stand the tension. Of the ten nurses who attended orientation to the surgical ICU with me, there were only two of us left. The others had moved on to less-demanding positions. Frankly, after a year in that pressure cooker, I was ready for a little break myself. So when Joyce asked me to come spend the summer with her and her kids, I jumped at the chance. At the time, giving up my paycheck didn't seem like such a big deal but the closer the time came, the more I wondered if I had planned well enough.

I could hear Kathy start to whimper on the other end of the line. I didn't want to come across as uncaring, but this was already getting to be a long and expensive phone call.

"Believe me, Kathy, it's not that I don't want to be in your wedding. I would love to. I just don't see how I can do it."

"I understand, Leslie." The way she said it, with deep hurt seeping through the brave façade, cut me like a knife. My mind was racing, grasping for a solution. Suddenly, I had a thought.

"Okay, wait a minute Kath, listen. Remember last weekend, when I was there visiting you, we went shopping at the mall in Desert Hot Springs and I bought that dress? You know, the cute blue one with the empire waist? Well, what if I got it back there to you – do you think you could return it for me and get my money back? That way I could use the money toward the bridesmaid dress instead."

"Leslie, that's a wonderful idea!" she said with revived enthusiasm. "Of course, I could do that for you.

In fact, Leila is going up to LA next weekend and she could pick it up and bring it back here."

Leila, Kathy and I, along with two other college friends, had shared an apartment together the summer before. Now Kathy and Leila were rooming together as they completed their first year of teaching in Palm Desert.

We finalized arrangements and I hung up the phone. I felt relieved at the solution we had come to. I really liked the dress I was giving up, but it was no substitute for Kathy's friendship. I was honored that she wanted me to be in her wedding. And so I resigned myself, once again, to playing the part of bridesmaid. But I had to wonder,

Will I ever have the leading role in a wedding?

I don't know why I was questioning it so much, considering my current situation. For five months I had been dating a guy from church who seemed like a very good possibility. Dale was a sporting goods salesman from Manhattan Beach. The fact that he had not graduated from college bothered me a little, but he didn't seem to let that stand in the way of success. He drove a fancy little sports car and owned his own ski boat. And, of course, he had all the latest and greatest sports gear. For Christmas he had surprised me with a fashionable and very expensive ski jacket made of real goose down. Dale really knew how to pamper a girl. We went out to eat at the nicest restaurants. Almost every weekend we were outdoors somewhere either skiing or hiking. We had lots of fun together. He was always such a gentleman, and my family just loved him. Recently, he had even made a point of letting me know about a diamond he had purchased and was keeping in his safe deposit box. I knew he was getting serious. Yet I found myself holding back.

Why did I refuse to give my heart completely to this wonderful guy?

"There it is. There's Makuma!" shouted Timmy.

Beneath us lay a long, narrow grass airstrip. Along one side ran a river and between the river and the airstrip was a clearing with a few buildings. Although I had never been to Makuma before, I had heard of it. GMU missionaries Ernest and Jean Johnson, with the help of some of the Shuar people, carved the station out of the rainforest thirty years before. It was an important crossroads for the Shuar as they walked the muddy trails from village to village. That made it the perfect place to teach the Shuar of the God who loved them and was willing to sacrifice His Son on their behalf.

Arlowe and Emma were excitedly pointing out landmarks to their two-year-old.

"Look, Timmy, there's our house. And the Hedlunds', and the Drowns'. See the river? And down there is where the hydro plant is. Can you see it?"

"Which house is Joyce's?" I blurted out, unable to contain my curiosity.

"Right there; the blue one next to our house; near the airstrip. See it?"

As I zeroed in on the corrugated roof of the house Emma was pointing out, I marveled at the emotions welling up inside of me. Somehow, despite the fact I had never even been here before, I felt as though I was coming home. It was crazy. I didn't even know Joyce and the kids all that well. Besides the few weeks I had spent with them in Yaapi, the only time I had seen them was at church during the nine months they spent back in California while John was receiving chemotherapy. The last time I had seen Joyce was at the funeral. Three months later she and the kids returned to the jungle. That was two years ago. So why did I feel such a close kinship with this courageous woman? Perhaps it was the warm welcome I had received on my previous visit. Or maybe it was the love she expressed to her family, to the Shuar and to me. It might have been due to the grace I observed in her as she endured the pain of watching her beloved husband succumb to the relentless cancer. Whatever the reason, now that I was here, I had no doubt that I was right where God wanted me at this time in my life.

Joyce had a wonderful openness to people, all people. I had seen her talking for hours to Shuar visitors in her home, listening to their stories, sharing in their laughter and their tears. My own story would be another for her to embrace. She loved romance and liked to keep tabs on the young men in my life. She asked insightful questions and I valued her opinion. Somehow, I felt, things would seem much clearer to me after talking with Joyce.

In any jungle village the sound of an approaching airplane brings people scurrying to the airstrip. As we began our landing, I caught sight of three towheads among the swarm of glossy black mops of hair hurrying in our direction. As soon as the propeller stopped spinning I jumped out and ran to meet them.

"Wow! You guys have gotten so big since last time I saw you." I hugged each of the Stuck kids. Don and Bob had grown a foot taller since last time I had seen them. Ruth, though tall for her nine years, still had the features of a little girl. "It's so nice to see you again."

Just then Joyce strode up, beaming her usual smile. I had wondered whether the events of the past few years would have taken their toll and dampened Joyce's innate joy of living. Any doubts I had vanished when I saw her radiant face.

"Leslie! Welcome! I can't believe you're here. It's wonderful."

She wrapped me in a bear hug. I felt swept up in the excitement of being back in the jungle with the people I loved.

Why did I enjoy being here so much? Was this God's way of telling me that this was the life for me? And, if so, where did Dale fit into all this?

I prolonged our hug a little, just to express the depth of feeling I had for this woman whom I admired so much. As we parted, she peered into my face.

"So, how are you doing, Leslie?"

"Fine," I answered, averting my gaze, afraid that my face would betray my inner feelings. I changed the subject to hide my discomfort.

"So, this is Makuma. I've heard so much about this place. Think I can get a tour?" I ended, directing my question to the kids.

"Can we take her to the river, Mom? Please. Please."

"There'll be plenty of time for that. First, let's help Leslie get her suitcases up to the house. Maybe after lunch we can swim."

I could tell by a subtle change in her voice that my attempt at distraction hadn't fooled Joyce. Sooner or later she would return to explore the crack that had opened in the door of my heart.

Joyce's house in Makuma was located on the second story of a cement block building in a clearing between the river and the airstrip. Several other similar homes, each brightly painted, rimmed the clearing. Closest to Joyce was the Beckers', and next to them on the other side was the home of Jim and Norma Hedlund. Jim, like Arlowe, was an electrical engineer. The Hedlunds had come to Makuma in 1972 to help install and maintain the new five-thousand-watt transmitter used for radio broadcasts.

On the opposite side of the clearing from Joyce lived Frank and Marie Drown in a house overlooking the river. The Drowns had lived in Makuma since before I was born. All of their children had been raised here. One of their sons, Tim, was back visiting for the summer. The Shuar language radio broadcasts from Makuma were the brain-child of Frank Drown. They began in 1962 with a small transmitter and battery-powered radio receivers built by HCJB engineers. The recent arrival of a larger transmitter led directly to Frank's latest project – building a hydroelectric plant on the Makuma River. The new transmitter used more energy and this was placing a strain on Makuma's diesel-powered generator. All the fuel to run the generator had to be flown in on MAF flights. Adding to the energy demands were the air-conditioned broadcasting studios located on the ground floor beneath Joyce's home. The controlled climate was necessary to protect the sensitive electronic equipment from the damaging humidity of the rain forest.

Upstairs in Joyce's home, though, it was sufficient to have ventilation provided by screened windows. The afternoon breeze gently ruffled the blue cotton print curtains adorning the kitchen windows.

"Recognize those?" asked Joyce, noticing that the curtains had caught my eye.

"Aren't they the ones I made for you in Yaapi?"

"That's right," she said. "I left most of the furnishings in the house in Yaapi – I still go back there to visit from time to time – but I brought out things that had special memories for me."

I was touched.

Joyce continued, "I was hoping you could do some sewing for me this time, too."

"I'd be happy to. What did you have in mind?"

"Well, the boys need new bathing suits. And Ruthie could stand some new dresses for school."

"Hmm, I don't know," I frowned in the direction of the kids, seated around the kitchen table, finishing their lunch. "I have some special memories of my own from my visit to Yaapi."

The kids exchanged knowing glances. Ruthie began to giggle.

"What?" demanded Joyce. "What are you laughing about?"

"Don't you remember, Mom?"

"Well, I certainly haven't forgotten," I assured them. "When I woke up after my first night in Yaapi, just as I was getting dressed, I remembered that John had told me to always shake out my shoes before I put them on just in case some critter had crawled into them during the night. So I did, and out popped the biggest, ugliest cockroach I had ever seen – what did you guys call them?"

"A shoot, a shoot!" they answered in gleeful unison.

"Yeah, well when the shoot came shooting out of my shoe, I looked up to see three giggling faces peeking in my door!"

"I hope you're not accusing my little angels," piped in Joyce with feigned indignation.

As our laughter faded, Don cried out while gazing through the window, "Hey, the Baltimore gang is heading to the river. Can we go?"

"Sure, go get your suits on." The kids disappeared in a flurry.

"So, who is this Baltimore gang I keep hearing about?" I asked. "Emma Becker mentioned them, too."

"Oh, Leslie, they are the neatest group of young people. They've been here about three weeks and have painted the entire hydro plant, inside and out, as well as several of the houses. They are such good workers and so much fun to have around. Unfortunately, they're leaving tomorrow. In fact, we're hosting a farewell dinner here for them tonight."

"What sort of a group are they?" I asked, trying to find out if there might be some young people around my age.

"I don't know. I'd guess most of them are in college."

I hoped Joyce wouldn't sense my disappointment at hearing that all of the guys would be younger than me.

"Leslie, why don't you go to the river with the kids?"

"But what about you, Joyce? Why don't I stay and help you?"

"No, no, I'm just going to be working on some radio programs this afternoon. You go and have fun with the young people."

"Well, okay, if you're sure?"

"I'm sure." She stopped what she was doing and looked right at me. "Go."

I knew enough from my time in Yaapi not to change into a bathing suit. Shuar culture prohibited a woman from revealing her thigh to public view. Exposing the breasts, on the other hand, was fine since they were only a means of delivering milk. I decided to keep both under wraps by wearing a pant-dress. It was a one-piece outfit with a sleeveless blouse on top and shorts below. My fashion ensemble was completed by a pair of matching, over-sized tennis shoes.

When we arrived at the river, the Baltimore gang was on the far side. Don untied a dugout canoe and gestured for me to get in.

"What about Bob and Ruthie?"

"I'll come back for them."

Don introduced me to everyone on the opposite bank, and then headed back across the river. Soon I was in the water, talking with a couple of the girls. Some of the boys were diving to the bottom of the river, seeing who could bring up the biggest rock. Suddenly, one of the guys broke the surface and sputtered:

"Oh no, I've lost my tooth!"

"What? What do you mean?"

"My bridge fell out!" he exclaimed, grimacing to show the gap where once had been his top left incisor.

Soon everyone, including the Stuck kids, joined the search. After twenty minutes of diving and hunting among the stones at the bottom of the river, the boy whose tooth was lost called off the search.

"It's okay," he said, determined not to spoil the fun for all the others. Then, fluttering his eyes and flashing a wide grin, he added, "Ain't I beautiful?"

Everyone howled. I was impressed with him. Realizing how important looks were to most people of his age, I admired his ability to make fun of himself and give everyone a laugh at his expense.

That night at the going-away dinner, members of the Baltimore gang provided the entertainment with singing, jokes and skits. The final skit involved the toothless boy, whose name was Steve, and one of the girls. They teamed up to create a miniature character with Steve's face. The character's legs were made from Steve's arms and the girl, standing behind Steve, provided the character's arms. The skit involved Steve observing, as he grinned from ear to ear, that he really should take better care of his teeth. "He" then proceeded to accomplish that feat by means of the girl's arms as she stood blindly behind him. Toothpaste was everywhere except in Steve's mouth. It went on until the audience was holding their sides, laughing, unable to catch their breath.

At the conclusion, Steve stood up and thanked each of the missionaries, by name, on behalf of the group, for all the hospitality and kindness they had shown. It was quite touching, and I noticed several of the missionaries had tears in their eyes.

As the last of our guests left, Joyce announced:

"Okay, kids, twenty minutes until they turn the generator off. Everybody into your PJ's and hop into bed. I'll be right in to pray with you."

The kids scurried off to obey. I started helping Joyce wash the dishes.

"I see what you mean about the Baltimore gang being so much fun," I began.

"Oh my word, wasn't that last skit hilarious? That guy, Steve, is a hoot – and so well-spoken, too."

"Yes," I agreed. "He seemed so mature for his age, so self-confident."

"In some ways he reminds me of John when we first met," Joyce said. A pregnant silence followed.

"Joyce? I don't want to be nosy, but I was wondering … what's it been like coming back here without John?"

"Very lonely," she admitted. "But the kids and the radio and my trips to out stations to visit church leaders keeps me busy and that helps me not to feel sorry for myself.

"But weren't you ever mad at God for taking John away?"

"Mad at God?" she asked, as though the thought had never crossed her mind. "No, Leslie. No. How could I be mad at God when it was Him who gave John to me in the first place?"

"Well, I had a hard time when John died." I admitted. "I felt angry at God. I kept thinking, 'Why, God? Why does it have to be John? There are so many mean people in the world who spend their lives focused on themselves. John was so capable and loved by the Indian people…and one of the few who knew the Shuar language. It doesn't make any sense. John spent his whole life serving You, and that's how You reward him? I just don't get it.'"

"Well, of course, I don't understand it either, Leslie, but I do know this. John and I had fifteen wonderful years together. A lot of people are married for a lifetime and never have fifteen years like we had. Living and working in the jungle allowed us to spend almost all our time together."

"I never thought about it that way."

"In some ways, John's death has made me better able to minister to others. Not that I would have ever chosen it in a million years." She paused. "For example, there's a preacher named Chiriap in a nearby community. He is such a neat man. He and his wife, Pauch, have two beautiful children, a boy and a girl. Last year, Pauch got bitten by a snake and died before we could get her to the hospital. Chiriap was devastated, as you can imagine. If it hadn't been for John's death, there's no way I could have understood what he was going through."

I marveled at her perspective. I was still mulling over what she had said when, without warning, she turned the course of the conversation in my direction.

"And what about you, Leslie? Is there a young man in your life?"

Without thinking, I started, "I've been dating a guy named Dale for a few months now."

I paused. Joyce's eyes were glued on me, waiting for me to continue. The floodgates were opened. Almost against my will I found myself pouring out my soul, telling Joyce everything about my relationship with Dale.

"I met him at church and we started doing things together with the career group in the beginning. He lives in Manhattan Beach and doesn't seem to mind the forty minute drive to see me. He comes almost every day. He'll take me out to eat or we'll get together with friends. We have many of the same interests. We went waterskiing right before I came here. He's lots of fun and recently has really gotten more serious about his relationship with the Lord."

"He sounds like a wonderful young man," Joyce concluded, once I paused long enough for her to respond.

"Yes, he is," I agreed. "That's the problem. There's really no good reason that I should be holding back."

"Except?"

"Except that I don't know that Dale is really interested in missions. I mean, he says he's interested, but I'm not sure he really understands what it means. I don't know that he has ever pictured himself living that way the rest of his life."

"Does he love you?"

"He says he does and I believe him. I think he loves me enough that he might be willing to tag along with me, but that's not what I want."

"Yes, you're right. It has to be something that comes from him."

"Oh, Joyce, I just don't know what to do. I feel like I'm standing at a crossroads. One way leads straight to love, marriage, a family. The other way isn't as clear. It seems like it would be harder and, if I'm honest, a bit scary. I feel like God is calling me down the second path. I just wish both paths met. I wish Dale could see how wonderful it is to serve God overseas."

"Well, why don't you invite him to come down here to find out?"

"Really, Joyce, really?" I shouted. "Could I?"

"I don't see why not. Now, first I'll have to check around to see where he can stay. Maybe the Beckers would be willing to put him up. Anyway, I'm sure we can work all that out."

"Oh, Joyce, that's wonderful." I was ecstatic. "I just know once he sees this place he'll fall in love with it."

"I sure hope so. But, Leslie, keep in mind," Joyce warned, "this kind of life is not for everyone. Not everybody takes to it the way you have."

"What do you mean? What's not to like?"

Just then, she reached across me and pointed to a large, hairy tarantula on the window sill in front of me. I screeched and jumped back away from the window as Joyce grabbed a broom. She approached the beast cautiously and then whacked it. I grimaced as she lifted the broom to reveal flattened legs lying at varying angles.

We looked at each other and laughed.

Chapter 5
Kevin's Epiphany

The morning after my arrival in Shell, I met another family that would impact my life profoundly. Following a sound night's sleep, I reported as instructed at 7am sharp to the upper apartment of a two-story concrete block building near the entrance to the hospital. This was the temporary home of Doug and Darlene Peters and their three elementary school-aged children. The Peters normally lived in Quito, but Doug had been asked to replace Norm Emery, the hospital administrator. Norm and his family were back in the U. S. on furlough for the summer. I would be having breakfast each morning with the Peters during the remaining weeks of their time in Shell.

The contrast with the Swanson household was immediately evident upon entering. Darlene was quiet, reserved and efficient. Doug was the outgoing personality, always looking for the humor in any situation. The whole tenor of the home was more sedate and orderly than what I had experienced the night before. The Peters' children – David, Debbie and Danny – sat quietly around the breakfast table while Doug read a selection from a little devotional book called *Our Daily Bread*. While we were eating, he would ask one or the other of the children a question related to that morning's reading. I was astounded by the intelligence and insight of their replies and subsequent discussion. Each interaction made evident the love and respect among all family members, one for another.

After breakfast, I met Doctor Swanson at the nurses' station to begin rounds. Doctor Swanson insisted I call him Wally. It was hard to get used to, but soon I noticed that all the nurses called him Wally. Wally Swanson was a remarkable man. A gifted clinician with a wealth of medical knowledge at his fingertips, he remained humble, unassuming and soft-spoken. It was easy to mistake his mild manner for insecurity or intellectual mediocrity – that is, until you spoke with him. His firmly-held ideas on all manner of subjects from medicine to religion were always well thought out and always presented unpretentiously.

Today was Tuesday. The surgeon on staff, Doctor John Doerfer, was already hard at work in the operating room. Wally and I made our way from room to room seeing all the hospitalized patients. Wally would talk to each one in Spanish and then translate for me, as he gently examined them. About half of the twenty or so patients were indigenous people and the other half were *mestizos*, of mixed indigenous and Hispanic ancestry. Wally told me that there were three culturally distinct indigenous groups who used the hospital. Each group- Quechua, Shuar and Waodani – had their own language, which sometimes made patient care challenging. A few of the indigenous men and most of the women could speak no Spanish, so Wally had to communicate with them as best he could.

Among the indigenous patients that day there was one Waodani. The rest were Shuar. Waodani, I was informed, was the more current name for the people formerly known as the Auca. I had read about the Auca and how fierce they were, so I was a bit surprised at the somewhat docile-appearing man I saw lying in bed with a patch over his empty eye socket. He certainly didn't look like a ruthless killer to me.

Wally explained to me that many of the diseases encountered at the Shell hospital were the same as conditions that might be found in the U. S. What made these cases more challenging was that, often, the people wouldn't come for treatment until the disease was far along in its progression. The reasons were many. The majority of the patients lived in very remote locations, requiring days of travel to see the doctor. Economics played a significant role in peoples' decisions of when to seek medical care. Each family had to take into account not just the cost of transportation and the cost of medical treatment, but also the impact of having to leave the family farm idle in order to accompany a family member to the hospital. Needless to say, people did not come for minor ailments. But, more than pure economics were involved. Some patients first sought the aid of *brujos*, or witchdoctors, and only came to the hospital as a last resort.

In addition to the familiar diseases, there were other conditions which physicians in a developed nation might well never see in a lifetime of practice. Many of these were unusual infectious diseases caused by parasitic worms.

The case that got my attention on rounds that day, though, was not caused by a parasite. As we approached one room, a strong, fetid odor reached us even before we entered. Inside the room, lying solemnly still in the bed, was a young Shuar woman. She obviously knew the routine of morning rounds, for as soon as she saw us, she pulled the sheets back discreetly to reveal a large, bulky dressing on her lower leg. There was an ominous green stain on the portion of the dressing over the outer aspect of her leg. As we approached, it became all too apparent that this was the source of the overpowering stench.

Oh, great. I know what my job's going to be.

One of the major reasons I disliked my surgery rotation in medical school, and discarded that specialty as a career option, was the amount of "scut work" involved.

Among the least favorite of those jobs was changing dressings on wounds that had become infected. Not only was it distasteful to handle the reeking dressings, but invariably terrible pain was inflicted on the patient. It was a necessary evil that no one enjoyed, and thus it fell to the junior person on the team, namely the medical student.

Much to my surprise, Wally collected the clean dressing materials himself and began gently removing the soiled bandage. The woman spoke no Spanish so lay stoically mute, allowing Wally to peel back the gauze which adhered to her outer leg. As he uncovered it, I tried very hard not to let the revulsion I was feeling show in my expression. Her entire lower leg from knee to ankle was filleted open. Yellow fat, pink muscle and white tendons were plainly visible. It looked like an illustration from an anatomy textbook. The foul, green liquid pooled in all the recesses and crevices. I waited until we were back out in the hall before asking Wally what on earth had caused such a devastating injury.

"Snakebite," he replied. "It's a big problem here, especially for the Indians. Most often they get bitten while clearing land for their crops. Since the women do most of the agricultural work, they're the ones affected most frequently. By the time they get here, there's not usually a lot we can do for them but watch for signs of infection and treat it when it happens. They tend to be terrible infections, like that girl's."

"Do people die from it?" I asked.

"Yes, but not often and not usually from infection. The other problem they have is that the venom can cause their blood to stop clotting, so they bleed. Most people who die from snakebite die from cerebral hemorrhage."

Silently, I wished there was something I could do to help them.

When we finished rounds, Wally led me to the end of the hall where the operating rooms were located. We changed into green scrub suits, then donned shoe covers, surgical caps and masks. Unlike in the U. S., where these last three items are made of paper and intended for disposal after a single use, here all were hand-sewn from worn cotton sheets. We entered the operating room where John Doerfer was placing sterile drapes on a patient in preparation for performing a Caesarean section. I noticed the drapes were also cloth rather than paper. Scurrying about the room was a very efficient Canadian nurse by the name of Beth Huddleston. She was teaching an Ecuadorian nurse, Irene, how to administer anesthesia. Helping John with the drapes was an Ecuadorian assistant who passed surgical instruments to John during the operation. Wally made the introductions and then excused himself to see patients in the clinic. I went out to the surgical sink to scrub my hands in anticipation of assisting John. Even the scrub brushes were non-disposable and had hard, sharp bristles. By the end of the required ten minute scrub my forearms were bright red. As I entered the operating room, John's assistant came to help me get into my sterile gown – cloth, of course. As I was waiting for her to hold open the sterile gloves for me to insert my hands, she instead reached to the table where she had her sterile instruments arranged. She retrieved a tin cup that looked like an over-sized salt shaker. Initially confused, I finally realized she wanted me to hold my hands out. When I did, she shook powdery corn starch out of the container onto my hands. She then reached for my sterile gloves and, as she held the first one out for me to place my hand in, it dawned on me what was going on. The ends of several of the fingers on the glove were patched with little squares of latex. Incredibly, even the gloves were re-sterilized and used over and over again. That's why the gloves didn't come pre-powdered as they did in the U. S. I felt embarrassed at the waste I had grown accustomed to.

John was waiting for me as I stepped to the operating table across from him. As soon as I was positioned, John took the scalpel and made a long incision along the lower portion of the woman's protuberant abdomen from one hip bone to the next. To my utter amazement I heard the patient speak in Spanish to Irene, the Ecuadorian nurse who was administering anesthesia.

"She's awake!" I whispered to John, pointing out the obvious.

"That's right." His voice was calm. "She has a spinal in. We don't like to give general anesthesia for C-sections. It could keep the baby from breathing well."

Relieved that the situation was under control, I returned my attention to the operation. I was fascinated by what I saw. John quickly but carefully opened each layer, exposing what lay beneath. Soon we had entered the abdomen and were separating the bladder from the front of the uterus. Next, John used the scalpel to make a hole in the lower portion of the uterus. As soon as he saw what looked like a water balloon bulge through the opening, he inserted his two forefingers and literally tore the uterus open. Immediately, the surgical field was flooded with blood mixed with clear fluid from the sac that had ruptured. I stood there aghast, not knowing what to do. John, seemingly unperturbed, simply reached inside the uterus with his right hand while pushing down on the woman's abdomen with his left. I'm not sure what I was expecting, but I was genuinely shocked to see a baby's head come out. Once the head appeared, John removed his hand from the woman's abdomen and grabbed the baby's head with one hand on each side of the face. He pulled the head down to one side and – pop! The baby sprang out like a jack-in-the-box. I stood there watching, totally enthralled. I was roused to action by the surgical assistant who tapped my hand insistently. I looked down to see her pushing a bulb syringe into my palm. Suddenly aware that I had been doing nothing to help, I used the syringe to suck out the baby's mouth and nostrils. Simultaneously, John was clamping and severing the umbilical cord. Irene poked her head over the drapes separating her from the surgical team and announced triumphantly "*varon!*" at which point the mother broke into tears. I looked questioningly at John.

"It's a boy," John explained.

That moment represented an epiphany for me. I really did love surgery! The reason I hadn't realized it until just then had to do with the lowly position occupied by medical students in the hierarchy of surgical education.

All surgical training programs are organized into teams. Each team consists of one or more fully-trained staff surgeons, a chief resident, a variety of junior residents at differing levels of training, one or more interns and, last but definitely least, the humble medical student. It is not that the medical student has no role on the team. In addition to being tasked with all the unpleasant jobs no one else wants to do, the medical student occupies a key position during teaching rounds. All questions regarding diagnosis and treatment of surgical patients begin by being directed to the medical student. These could range from the purely factual -"What's the patient's most recent serum sodium level?"- to truly philosophical questions that fully trained and board certified surgeons can't agree on. No one expects the medical student to actually know the answer to a question, but everyone enjoys the spectacle of watching the pitiable wretch writhe in agony beneath the microscope of disdain. Most humiliating of all is that this interrogation is carried out at the patient's bedside, exposing the medical student for the imposter that he is. Although some patients are sympathetic, most soon learn that they, too, can entirely disregard the inconsequential medical student.

On the rare occasions when the student is allowed into the Holy of Holies, the operating room, he or she maintains a position at the far end of the operating table, bent in an awkward position, trying to hold a retractor motionless for hours on end. Heaven forbid that he should ever actually see what is taking place, let alone get his hands inside a living human body.

After lunch, John and I joined Wally in the outpatient clinic. The waiting room was full of people waiting to be seen or else accompanying family members. I stayed with John or Wally as they went from room to room evaluating patients. I tried to tune my ear to hear and understand what the patients were saying, but I usually had to ask for translation.

Dr. Wally Swanson and Kevin at the outpatient clinic

The pharmacy, laboratory and x-ray departments were all located in the outpatient wing. Virtually every patient made a stop by the lab to turn in a stool sample before being seen by the doctor. It was regarded as one of the vital signs: pulse, temperature, blood pressure, stool exam. Zulay, the Ecuadorian woman who worked in the lab, showed me several of the specimens under the microscope. I was familiar with what the various worm eggs looked like from parasitology classes in undergraduate and medical schools, but I still was amazed by the sheer number and variety recovered. After all, these weren't some stale samples used year after year in a classroom. The little beasts we were seeing had just come from these living, breathing human beings in the clinic. Virtually every specimen examined had eggs of at least one parasite. One specimen I saw from a little girl had five different varieties!

Zulay doubled as an x-ray tech for purposes of after-hours coverage, so she was only too happy to show me how to use the antiquated x-ray equipment. The x-ray unit itself was a World War II vintage portable machine. This was handy, because it meant it could be wheeled from its usual location in the outpatient clinic to the ward or operating room as needed. The x-ray films were encased in large metal cassettes. The body part to be x-rayed was placed between the cassette and the head of the machine. Once everything was properly positioned, a chart was consulted which detailed the proper kilovolts and milliamperes to be dialed into the machine, depending on the type of x-ray being taken. The operator then stepped behind a lead shield and shouted "*No respire, no respire*" to the patient, while pressing down on the firing button attached to the machine by a cord. After shooting the film, the cassette was retrieved and taken into the dark room to be developed. The cramped space of the dark room smelled strongly of the ammonium and sodium bromide and acetic acid used in the developing process. Everything was done by feel. The cassette was opened by turning the metal clasps and the film removed, with care being taken to touch only the edges. The film was then attached to a large metal frame by clips along its border. This assembly was submerged in a series of chemical baths to develop and rinse the image. Within a few days I was proficient enough to save Zulay some trips in from home at night.

By the third day at the hospital I was beginning to understand and fit into the pattern of life at Epp Memorial. Monday, Wednesday, Friday and Saturday began with morning rounds followed by outpatient clinic. Tuesday and Thursday mornings were reserved for scheduled operative cases, with clinic in the afternoons. Superimposed on this routine were emergency cases which could show up any time of day or night. Some of these cases required urgent operations. I was just beginning to feel comfortable in my role as helper in the process when, after rounds one morning, Wally announced.

"John is out sick today. We've got a big clinic, so I'll need your help. I'll take these two rooms. You see patients in that room and let me know if you have any questions."

My face remained impassive as my stomach churned. Not only was I not a doctor, I couldn't speak the language.

Yeah, I have a question. Is Wally out of his mind?

With resignation, I entered my assigned exam room and opened my *Spanish Medical Vocabulary* book, trying desperately to memorize it before the first patient showed up. That day I did a lot of listening and sign language. I examined each patient from head to foot, because I usually had no clue as to why they had come to see the "doctor".

John was out for three days with the flu. It turned out to be the best thing that could have happened to me. I developed a routine by memorizing a series of questions that required "yes" or "no" answers and did not allow the conversation to stray. Once John returned, I continued seeing patients on my own, asking help from Wally or John as needed. For the first time in my life I actually felt like a real doctor. It was intoxicating.

Chapter 6
Leslie's Turmoil

The soft brown eyes twinkled from within the frame of jet black hair. Chiki suppressed a self-conscious laugh, covering her mouth with one hand while still clutching the cloth on the sewing table with the other. She was finding it very difficult to co-ordinate feeding the material into the threaded needle, while at the same time maintaining the proper foot rhythm to keep the treadle sewing machine running smoothly. As I stood behind her and helped guide the material, I was struck by how similar we were and, yet, how different. My arm and hand on the sewing surface next to hers shared identical form and function. It was true that next to hers, my skin appeared almost chalky, despite my being known among friends back home as having an olive complexion. But aside from this shade of difference, our moving parts were more or less interchangeable. Yet between us there yawned a chasm, a chasm of language and culture, a chasm we were both making efforts to bridge. Smiles went a long way toward closing that gap.

Chiki's gentle and kind manner belied her cultural heritage. Like all Shuar, Chiki lived a difficult life. Much effort is spent in trying to pry today's meal from a begrudging forest. While the men hunt and fish, the women tend the sparse gardens of yuca and plantain. Often, Shuar men have several wives, all living in the same household. Wives are expected to do most of the heavy labor while the men sit around socializing, sharing stories of hunting and war. In Shuar culture, women are viewed more as possessions than partners.

The spirit world is very real to the Shuar. The practice of witchcraft is common and credited with causing illness and even death. One result of this belief system is a cycle of revenge killings. If a relative of mine dies, I would seek out the enemy who, obviously, had hired a *brujo* to poison my family member with magic darts. Once identified, I am honor bound to kill him and any of his family who might get in my way. His relatives, then, would not rest until they had gotten revenge on me and my family. It is a horrible, fearful way to live.

The only hope for interrupting that cycle is the good news of reconciliation. God has reconciled man to Himself through the sacrifice of His Son. As a result, man can be reconciled to man through forgiveness for wrongs done. That is the simple message of hope preached to the Shuar by the early missionaries. It had revolutionized Shuar culture for those who believed, ending the cycle of revenge and murder. Now, Shuar Christians were being trained to spread the same message via radio waves to their brothers scattered throughout the rain forest.

Chiki, eight years my junior, lived with Joyce in order to be able to attend the health promoter course in Makuma. Health promoters are taught basic principles of hygiene and medical treatment. They provide the first level of health care for their communities. While attending the course, Chiki helped pay for the cost of room and board by doing odd jobs around the house and helping Joyce prepare radio programs.

When Chiki saw me sewing dresses for Ruthie, she asked through Joyce if I would be willing to teach her. I was only too happy to agree. She was cheerful, helpful and easy to be around. As we worked together, I wondered why God had decided to place me in a loving, Christian family in America rather than out here, each day fearing the revenge of my enemies and their spirit-allies. It was too mind-boggling to think about right now. I decided to stick to the task at hand.

"That's right, Chiki. Now you're getting it," I said, hoping the tone of my voice would convey the message that my words could not.

"So, how's the project coming along?" Joyce asked as she entered the room.

"Pretty well. It took a little while, but I think Chiki's really catching on now."

"Oh, good."

Joyce said something to Chiki in Shuar. She responded by lowering her head as she glanced up at me in what was easily translatable to English as "Aw, shucks".

"Well, I hate to interrupt progress, but it's time for Chiki to go to class. And I've got to go down to the studio to work on some radio programs. Leslie, would you mind doing some wash while we're gone?"

"Not at all, I'd be happy to."

"Have you ever used a wringer washing machine?"

"No, but I'm sure I can learn."

She showed me an aluminum tub that was elevated on wheeled legs. Suspended on vertical braces attached to the tub was the wringer. It consisted of two rollers, each about the size and shape of a rolling pin, located one above the other. Attached to one of the rollers was a small electric motor that allowed you to wring the sudsy water out of the clothes as you fed them between the rollers. Next to the machine were several aluminum wash tubs. One of them was filled with clean water. Clothes plucked from the sudsy wash water were put through the wringers and allowed to fall into this tub for rinsing. With a final wringing after rinsing, the clothes were ready to dry.

"Where's the dryer?" I asked, looking around the room.

"Right over here," Joyce indicated through the open window.

Just outside the back door was a pulley with a rope running through it and across the grassy yard below, to another pulley fixed to the antenna for the radio station.

"Just be sure to keep an eye on the weather and gather the laundry in, if it looks like rain. Oh, yes, and be careful of any buttons as you put them through the wringer. If they're not flat, they can break. Bye now. See you in a couple of hours."

With that, she was out the door. I filled the tub and began agitating the dirty laundry in the water.

This is pretty easy.

But then, as I began wringing the clothes between cycles, I saw a shirt button turn up on its side and pop off. By the time I stopped the wringer, a second button had broken in two. After that, I took more care to feed in the buttons horizontally but, in doing so, I kept getting my fingers pinched between the rollers. As I looked at the remaining piles of dirty laundry, I realized I had a lot of work ahead of me. The air was thick and perspiration beaded on my forehead. After several hours of hard work, I got all the clothes washed, wrung out and hung on the line.

Whew. That took longer than I thought it would.

I made myself a cup of tea and settled onto the couch with a copy of Frank Drown's newly published book, *Mission to the Headhunters*. Soon, I was deeply involved in Frank's account of walking the trails into Makuma in the days before air travel was available in this part of the world. I found it fascinating. All of a sudden, my concentration was broken by the sound of feet coming up the steps. As my reverie was interrupted, I became aware of a loud rat-a-tat-tat on the tin roof.

"The laundry!" I screamed as I ran to the door; but, it was too late. Everything was wetter than when I had hung it out.

"Joyce, I am so sorry."

"It doesn't matter. The sun will come out again."

"But, that's not all. I broke off several of the buttons."

"Leslie, we can sew more buttons on. I think I have some in my sewing box. Don't worry about it."

One of the many qualities that attracted me to Joyce was her ability to put people at ease, even when they had messed up. She never made me feel small or stupid for mistakes that I made. And I made more than my share.

One morning Joyce and I were up early, fixing breakfast for the kids. I sliced one of the loaves of bread that we had baked the night before. As always, I struggled to make the slices even. Next, I used a small glass to cut a hole in the center of several slices. These were placed in a frying pan with butter melted in the bottom. I broke an egg into each cutout hole and fried them up. "Egg-in-a-hole" was a favorite of the kids. Lately, I found myself enjoying them, even though I had never been fond of eggs.

Meanwhile, Joyce was using the other loaf to fix a picnic lunch for us. We had made plans to hike to the "butterfly rock" further up the Makuma River, where butterflies congregated. I had made each of the Stuck kids a butterfly net using a stick, a coat hanger and some netting. We were anxious to try them out. The rainforest is home to a wide variety of beautiful butterflies. My favorite memento of my previous visit to Ecuador was a collection of butterflies I had caught. They were mounted on a cotton background in a plain wooden frame hand-made by John Stuck. He had presented it to me as a gift when we left Yaapi.

Joyce opened a tin of tuna fish and then walked over to the kerosene-powered refrigerator. She rummaged through the containers within.

"Now what did I do with that mayonnaise?"

I winced. "Uh, Joyce, I'm afraid I had that on my sandwich last night before I went to bed," I confessed.

"All of it?"

"Uh, yeah, actually. I kind of have this thing against dry sandwiches," I said.

I felt terrible, knowing that Joyce couldn't just go out and buy more mayonnaise. Nearly everything we ate or drank had to be made from scratch. Even the simplest meal required a lot of planning ahead.

"No problem." she reassured me. "I'll just make some more real quick."

She cracked an egg into the blender, added some vinegar and mustard and turned the blender on. As she began slowly adding oil, she suddenly remembered something.

"Oh, Leslie. In the fridge is a container of *naranjilla* juice to have with breakfast. It needs to have sugar added. Could you do that while I'm finishing up here?"

"Of course."

I was happy for a chance to redeem myself. *Naranjilla* is a small, tropical fruit; one of the few crops that can readily be grown in the rain forest. I grabbed the juice from the fridge and chose the sugar from the row of yellow graduated- sized Tupperware containers on the kitchen counter. Like everything else in the jungle, sugar had to be protected from the ever-present moisture and insects. I added three heaping scoops to the pitcher, stirred it and set it on the table.

"Time for breakfast," called Joyce. "Come and get it."

One by one, the kids paraded in, rubbing their bleary eyes.

After saying grace, Don poured himself a glass of juice and, gulping down a big mouthful, suddenly jumped up and darted to the kitchen sink where he spit it all out.

"Mom, are you trying to kill us?"

Immediately, Bob and Ruthie each stuck a finger in the juice and placed it on their tongues. "Yuck!" they grimaced.

Joyce, guessing what had happened, asked, "Leslie, which container of sugar did you use?"

When I showed her, she said, "Taste it."

Sure enough, it was salt, not sugar. I now remembered how, when I first arrived in the jungle, I was surprised by the appearance of the sugar. It was coarse and grainy with a yellowish tint, not at all like the fine, white crystals I was used to.

I felt so bad; not only about the expense of buying the *naranjilla,* but also all the time and effort it took for Joyce to cut them, scoop out the seeds, squeeze and strain the juice and then boil the water to add. I began apologizing, but she would have none of it.

"Ha! That's a great joke. She really got us on that one, didn't she kids?"

Soon we were all laughing. I loved being with this wonderful family. And I loved this life. It's true that it took a lot more effort just to accomplish the day-to-day tasks of living, but I even enjoyed the work of it. And life sure wasn't all work. Hardly a day went by that we weren't swimming or fishing at the river. Often we would hike for hours through muddy quagmires to visit believers in other communities. Even though I could hardly understand a word that was said, I never tired of speaking my limited Shuar to the women and playing with the children while I waited for Joyce to finish encouraging the Shuar. There was such a mutual love and respect between them. At the end of each visit, in the evenings when we were back at her home, Joyce would share with me the struggles that the Shuar in the various villages were experiencing.

"Mitiap, the man we met in Ayui today, told me that his leg has started draining pus again. He has such a good spirit about it, but I know he's worried. And, I'm really concerned for the believers in Kumbantsa. Their leader, Awananch, is getting married soon and he plans to move to another village after the wedding. That will leave the church in Kumbantsa without any mature believer to lead them. Leslie, let's pray."

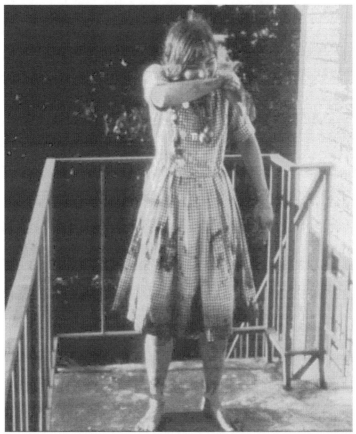

Leslie returns to Makuma from a jungle hike

Leslie with an elderly Shuar woman

We would spend time praying for each of the concerns. I appreciated Joyce including me. It really allowed me to feel a part of building God's church in the *Oriente*. It was like a dream come true for me. Working hard, having fun and contributing to something of eternal value. How could life get any better or more fulfilling?

About three weeks into my time in Makuma, we visited Yaapi, the village where I had stayed with the Stucks on my first trip to Ecuador. It was a wonderful time of reminiscing about those happy, carefree days before John's cancer recurred.

The night we returned to Makuma, however, my heart was in turmoil. Perhaps the bittersweet memories that had been stirred were the cause, but for whatever reason, I was feeling very introspective that night as I was getting ready for bed. I was so disappointed to find that there was still no letter from Dale waiting for me on my return to Makuma. I felt cut off and isolated. There was no telephone or television connecting Makuma with the outside world. Communication was limited to daily radio contacts with the other jungle stations.

Mail service was irregular and dependant on MAF flight schedules.

Still, it had been three weeks since I left California, and that should have been plenty of time for a letter to arrive. I had already gotten a letter from my roommate, Ruth. She wrote to confirm the details of her flight arrival in Quito. Like me, Ruth graduated from the nursing program at Biola. After graduation, we worked at the same hospital. Ruth had begun her nursing career on a medical floor but had recently transferred to the pediatric ward. She, too, had an interest in missions and I encouraged her to take advantage of my presence in Ecuador in order for her to check out missionary nursing for herself. In just a few days, Joyce, the kids and I would be traveling up to Quito to put the kids in the dorm for the school year. At the same time we would meet Ruth as she arrived and bring her back down to Makuma with us.

As I pulled my nightgown over my head and let it fall into place around me, my mind began to wander where I didn't want it to go.

Ruth! She was pretty, fun, currently unattached and definitely interested in guys. She and Dale were friends and she had mentioned in her letter that they had gone out to eat together after I left. Neither of them had ever given me cause to be jealous before, but now ...? What if Dale had started liking Ruth? Is that why I hadn't heard from him? Was he not man enough to tell me himself? Was he going to let Ruth drop the bomb when she arrived this week?

I sat down on my bed and pulled the socks off my feet. My mind swirled with questions and uncertainties. My stomach churned as fear gripped me. I struggled to make reason rule over emotion.

Is God calling me to be a missionary nurse, or not? I believe, now more than ever, that He is. But, what if things don't work out with Dale? Am I supposed to go alone? If I go off to some remote location as a single woman, what are the chances I will ever meet someone I can share my life with? Am I willing to trust God enough for that?

I was scared.

What's the big deal? There are quite a few single women I've met in Ecuador. They seem to be content. But then, recently one of them confided to me that she struggles with loneliness and still holds out hope that God will provide her with a partner. I certainly don't want to be 50 years old and still looking for a mate!

My stomach tightened.

"Lights out in five minutes!" Joyce called from her room next door.

I'm strong and independent. If anybody can make it as a single, I can. But I have to admit that my deep desire is to have a family of my own. That desire has only been reinforced by these weeks I've spent with Joyce and her kids. Look at me! I 'm already twenty-four years old. It's high time I start a family of my own, instead of living vicariously through Joyce, enjoying **her** *children and* **her** *ministry.*

I could feel myself begin to shake. It wasn't that I was cold. It was what I did when I was really tense or talking to someone about something very important. My thoughts swirled as I grasped at something to make sense out of the way I was feeling.

Lord what do you want from me?

I know the promise from Scripture: "Delight yourself in the Lord and He will give you the desires of your heart." But, what does that mean for me, right here, right now? It sounds like You're willing to fulfill my desire. But what does it mean for me to delight myself in You? Aren't I already doing that? What more do You want? I want to be obedient, but what am I supposed to do?

I lay there, thinking, as the generator powered down and the lights dimmed. Agitated, I fumbled for the matches and the candle on my bedside table. As the glow of the candle lit the room enough for me to see my Bible, I grabbed it and pulled it into bed with me. Flipping the pages open to Psalm 37, I searched to see if there was something I was missing.

It was true, just as I had remembered it. The verse really did say that if I delighted myself in God, He would give me the desires of my heart. But was I willing to delight myself in Him without a husband? Of course, I knew that marriage was no guarantee of happiness. There were married people I knew who were unhappy. But I also realized that I did not like being alone. Raised as an only child for the first eight years of my life, I had always wished I had a brother or sister and was thrilled when my parents adopted my brother, Brian. I liked being with people and was always looking for friends. That was one thing I had loved at college – there were always people around. The abundance of people meant the possibility of many friends. Since I never had a sister, I spent hours talking with girlfriends in the dorm sharing in their hopes, dreams and disappointments. Sure, sometimes there were conflicts and difficulties with roommates, but I had also learned from each relationship and enjoyed the interaction that living in close quarters affords. The thought of going alone to a foreign country, living among people of another language and culture with no one to talk to sounded like a huge, insurmountable mountain to climb. Was I willing to do this?

Yes, it had been wonderful sharing Joyce's life here in the jungle but that couldn't go on indefinitely. Sooner or later I would have to decide what I was going to do with my life. My eyes drifted down to the next verse: "Commit your way to the Lord, trust also in Him, and He will do it."

I had committed my way to the Lord, but was I trusting in Him? Or, was I dictating what I wanted and expecting God to do it? I was stung by the realization that maybe I wasn't really trusting God at all. I wanted Him to do what I wanted rather that trusting in Him to do what He considered best for me. Maybe I didn't want to let go of what I had until God showed me something better in exchange. That wasn't trusting God at all. It dawned on me that I needed to place my full confidence in God – not in marriage or in Dale or in a career, but in God and in whatever He had for me.

How could I have been so blind?

Lying there in bed with tears welling up in my eyes, I poured out my heart to God:

Lord, help me. I'm scared. I believe that You called me to serve You overseas, but I don't know if I can do it alone without a husband. And yet, I know I've always been pretty independent...self sufficient. I'm probably more able to go it alone than some. I know You are with me, I want to serve You, but I just don't know if now is the right time. What if Dale's lost interest in me? Or what if he comes down here and doesn't really like it? Then what am I supposed to do? Break up with him? Maybe I will never be satisfied with any guy. Maybe I'm being too picky. Maybe no man can measure up to what I want.

In my mind I know I can trust You, but it's just so hard. Are You asking me to go to the mission field alone? In my heart I desire a family, but not if that isn't what You want for my life. I know that You know what is best for me. Forgive me for not trusting You more. If You really want me to go to the mission field alone, I'm willing to do it. But...I need for You to show me beyond any shadow of a doubt that's what You want. I can't do it unless there is no doubt in my mind.

So please, please show me very clearly if I am supposed to break off my relationship with Dale. And then, give me the strength to do it. You know how scary this is for me. Dale may be my last chance at marriage and a family. But more than marriage or anything else, Lord, I want to do what You want me to do. Thank You for being patient with me. I do trust You, Lord. Thank You for loving me. Thank You for guiding me even though I don't know the future. To me the way seems uncertain, but I am in Your hands. Do with me what you want. I'm trusting You with my hopes, my fears, my dreams, my future, yes, my very life. It's all Yours Lord. I give You all!

My head rested on my pillow. My trembling had stopped. I sensed His presence, His love. My troubled heart was at peace, I blew out the candle and stared into the darkness. The fight was over. I knew I couldn't be in a safer place.

Chapter 7
Kevin's Invitation

There was no shortage of work to do at the hospital. Still, time was allotted for fun. On my first free afternoon, Jeff Swanson invited me to join a group of friends going swimming in the Alpayacu River. The Alpayacu was located between Shell and Mera. There were closer swimming holes, but the attraction of the Alpayacu was its bridge. The main road from Baños crosses the Alpayacu a few hundred yards from where that small tributary empties into the Pastaza River. We unloaded from the car and stood atop the bridge, peering over the side at the river thirty feet below. At that point the Alpayacu looks like little more than a stream, perhaps ten yards across. Without warning, Jeff launched himself over the railing head first. I was about to run down to the water's edge to haul his paralyzed body from the river when his head bobbed to the surface, laughing.

"Come on in. It's great."

I remained skeptical as one after another of the kids that were with us jumped, laughing and screaming, into the trickle below. Finally, I was left alone on top of the bridge.

"Don't worry. It's deeper than it looks," they all assured me.

I stood on the rail and looked down. I have a fear of heights. No way did I want to do this. But they were little kids, for crying out loud.

"Move over a little to your left," Jeff advised. "If you land too far right you'll break your neck."

"Great," I muttered as I shuffled left. I closed my eyes and dove into emptiness. The shock of the cold mountain run-off took my breath away but, to my surprise, I survived. I even repeated the performance a couple more times to prove it wasn't a fluke.

On the ride home Jeff admitted to me that this was an initiation they put all new medical students and other visitors through, in order to prove their mettle.

"Earlier this summer we had a student from Georgia here," Jeff related. "We brought him out here and were looking up at him, laughing and making fun of him. All of a sudden, he did a handstand on the rail and executed a perfect triple gainer. The joke was on us. He had been a state diving champ!"

I couldn't top that, but at least I had escaped the Alpayacu with both my life and my manhood still intact.

With no television available, we spent our evenings playing games at the Swansons' house or reading. I devoured everything I could get my hands on about the history of this place— *Jungle Pilot, Shadow of the Almighty, Through Gates of Splendor, The Dayuma Story.* I was fascinated by the true tale of five young friends plotting together to bring the gospel to the unreached and hostile Waodani, or Aucas, as they were then known. One of the group's leaders, MAF pilot Nate Saint, had lived in Shell. It was from here that the five took off on their secretive flight eighteen years before. None of them returned, all speared to death by the people they had gone to help. But the story didn't end there. What made it truly remarkable was what happened following their deaths. Nate Saint's sister, Rachel, and Elizabeth Elliot, who was married to one of the men, entered the tribe a few years later. They had learned the Waodani language from a tribeswoman who had escaped the deadly vortex of revenge killings. The women, accompanied by Elizabeth's infant daughter, Valerie, succeeded in bringing the message of God's love for all men to the killers. To this day, Rachel Saint lived among the very people who had speared her brother to death. I found it an inspiring story of altruistic love. I was curious to find out what could motivate people to accomplish such acts of selfless giving.

One evening I found myself standing on the veranda of the Fuller house talking about the day's events with John Doerfer. Out of the blue, he asked me if I had ever read the Bible. I replied that I was familiar with its general contents. He challenged me to open its pages and investigate it further. Not wanting to provoke a disagreement, I allowed as how that would probably be a good idea, though I did not really intend to do so.

Later that evening, my conscience began to get the better of me. I was afraid John might ask me the next day what I thought of it. Not wanting to disappoint him, I opened the Bible he had lent me and found the portion that he had recommended, the book of Romans. To my way of thinking, it started out as pretty slow reading, with a lot of stuff about how an angry God was going to punish bad men. Things like: "But because of your stubbornness and unrepentant heart you are storing up wrath for yourself in the day of wrath and revelation of the righteous judgment of God." It seemed like the usual scare tactics the priests and nuns I had known employed to keep everybody in line. Then there was a whole long section about the Jews and how they were just as bad off as the rest of us since, even though God had given them the law, none of them, "not even one," does good. It all sounded pretty depressing. But then came a passage talking about how there was a righteousness apart from the law for all those who believe in Jesus Christ. It ended up by saying: "Where then is boasting? It is excluded … for we maintain that a man is justified by faith apart from works of the Law." That caught my attention. It was a new concept to me. My understanding of how things worked was that, when you died, there was some kind of cosmic scale that measured the good you had done versus the bad, to see if you had earned the right to heaven. But this passage I just read seemed to be turning that whole system upside down. I figured I would need to give this new idea some more thought. On the face of it, it didn't seem very logical or fair. Why would God allow someone into heaven if they weren't good?

In the meantime, though, there was another long, boring section having something to do with Abraham. I was just about ready to call it quits for the night, figuring I had read enough to fake my way through any follow-up discussion, when the writer all of a sudden went back to talking about being justified by faith. I decided to read on a little further. That's when I came upon the following passage:

> For while we were still helpless, at the right time Christ died for the ungodly. For one will hardly die for a righteous man; though perhaps for the good man someone would dare even to die. But God demonstrates His own love toward us, in that while we were yet sinners, Christ died for us.

I closed the Bible and put it down. My thoughts were churning.

Maybe that explains why the five missionaries were willing to die. They were trying to copy Christ who 'died for the ungodly.' Well, it makes sense, sort of. He was a great teacher and left us quite an example to follow. Still, it seems pretty fanatical.

Thoughts such as these floated, weightless and random, through my brain. I tried to organize and prioritize them but, in the midst of doing so, drifted off to sleep.

Aside from traveling through the pages of books, my world was pretty confined during those days. Life was spent between my apartment, the hospital, the Peters' house for breakfast, and many evenings spent with the Swansons. You could stand at any one of those places and hit the others with a well-thrown rock.

Game nights at the Swanson house were always raucous affairs with lots of laughter. Often the conversation would get around to God, usually directed by Charlotte. These people were definitely different. For them, God was a normal, natural part of their everyday lives, not some distant deity you had to pay homage to every Sunday. They thought nothing of inserting God into the most mundane conversation. Mercifully, no one confirmed my worst fears by whacking me over the head with a Bible. Any pressure I might have felt was self-induced.

One evening, Charlotte asked, "Kevin, why did you go into medicine?"

Not wanting to open the door too wide, I gave her the short version, "I want to help people."

"That's nice, but why?"

"I don't know. It just seems like the right thing to do."

I didn't really feel like letting Charlotte know the whole story. The truth of it was that my interest in becoming a doctor began while I was still in my chubby, timid, pre-pubescent stage. I was a voracious reader, living an imaginary life of adventure through the stories I read. One book in particular, or rather a trilogy of books, fired my imagination. It was a true account by Dr. Tom Dooley of his experiences as a young Navy physician. The ship he was stationed on rescued Vietnamese refugees fleeing from the communist forces following the French defeat at Dien Bien Phu. Later, he returned to set up clinics to care for people displaced from their homes by the war. His story of selfless devotion inspired me. I pictured myself caring for sick and hurting people who had nowhere else to turn. I could just imagine the profound and eternal gratitude of those whose lives I snatched from the jaws of death, not to mention the admiration of my peers for my altruistic service to mankind.

Gradually, that noble vision became lost in the frantic activity of cramming for tests and writing papers in undergraduate school. But there was more to it than just the effort required to maintain a high enough GPA to be accepted to medical school. Deep down I realized that somewhere along the way I had lost the sense of purpose that had sparked my determination to become a doctor. In medical school I just drifted along, taking the required courses. By the time my classmates and I approached our senior year we were allowed quite a bit of flexibility in scheduling elective courses in various areas of particular interest to us. As I opened the course catalog to check out my choices, there it was – "Tropical Medicine Elective". The words jumped off the page. "Spend three months working at a jungle hospital in Ecuador." Without hesitation I registered for the class. I think somehow I was hoping it would re-ignite in me a passion for helping others and give meaning to my life.

"What if the people you're trying to help don't appreciate what you're doing for them, maybe even resent it?"

It was as though Charlotte was reading my thoughts. I realized I had no answer.

"I don't know. I haven't really thought about that," I answered, as I short-circuited the conversation by chasing after one of the kids.

Later that night, when I was alone in my room, I wondered about Charlotte's question. I knew in my heart that she was right. If I was serious about practicing medicine in a place like this, I would need more motivation than just being admired and appreciated by the people I was treating. But what could provide such motivation? I had no answer.

Sunday mornings were reserved for services at *Luz del Evangelio* church, which I attended regularly despite not understanding a word of what was spoken or sung. I endured it for the sake of what came next. After church, all the missionaries would pile into whatever vehicles were available and head into Puyo. With a population approaching five thousand, Puyo was considered the big city compared to Shell. It was also the capital of Pastaza province, so it was where one went for government business or shopping. On Sundays, however, the destination was the restaurant of the Hotel Europa. There they served a delicious lunch with a fixed menu which never varied. The meal began with *locro*, a thick potato soup with slices of hard-boiled eggs and half an avocado floating on top. Next, came the main course of roasted chicken and rice with a side order of vegetables served cold in the Ecuadorian style. No one I knew ever ate the vegetables for fear of contracting some dreaded tropical disease. In truth, had people not studiously avoided peeking in the kitchen, they probably would have avoided the entire meal. Still, it made a nice break in the routine. There was always plenty of friendly, easy banter around the table. Life was good.

The first hint that this idyllic existence would not continue forever came the beginning of August. The Emerys came back from furlough, freeing the Peters to return to their home in Quito. With the Peters gone, I now took my breakfast in the little kitchen building next to the hospital. I missed the fun times spent around the table with Doug and Darlene and their family.

The other change that was occurring was that the Swansons were packing up their house, preparing to move to Quito. After twelve years in Shell, Wally and Char felt it was time to move on to where they could be with their children during the high school years. Classes were due to begin the middle of August. Charlotte would move to Quito with the children, while Wally remained behind to await the arrival of his replacement. The house they were building on the outskirts of Quito was nearly completed. I was relieved that Wally wouldn't be leaving prior to my departure.

Whether influenced by the changes that were occurring or by the reading I had been doing, I began to dream of further adventures and experiences. I asked Wally about the possibility of getting out to one of the Indian villages to see what life was like in the rain forest. He promised he would give it some thought and ask around. I let it drop, knowing he would keep his word.

On the Monday morning after Charlotte and the Swanson kids had left for Quito, I joined Wally in the hospital kitchen for breakfast. Wally's brow was uncharacteristically furrowed.

"What's wrong?" I asked, thinking that perhaps one of our patients had taken a turn for the worse overnight.

"This arrived on that flight that came down from Quito yesterday evening", he replied, as he pushed a newspaper across the Formica table top toward me.

It was a ten-day-old copy of the Miami Herald. Across the front page, in large, bold print, the headlines screamed:

NIXON RESIGNS

Well, good. Now, at last, maybe we can get this whole Watergate mess behind us.

I was about to share my opinion as to how President Nixon had gotten just what he deserved for his lying and hypocrisy; but before I had a chance to get started, we were interrupted.

The screen door opened and in walked three strangers, all *gringas*. I was immediately attracted to the two younger women. They both appeared about my age. One had long, dark, straight hair and a turned-up nose. The other had long, blonde hair with bangs just touching her dark eyebrows. Beneath the arc of those eyebrows were two of the biggest, prettiest hazel eyes I had ever seen. Both of the younger women were slender and attractive.

"Hi, Wally," exclaimed the oldest of the three women.

"Hello, Joyce. This is a surprise. What are you doing here?"

"We're just on our way back to Makuma from Quito. We've been up there putting the kids in the dorm. Have you met Leslie Williams? She's been staying with me this summer."

The blonde stepped forward to shake hands. "Nice to meet you, Dr. Swanson. I've heard a lot about you," she said.

"Wally, please," he responded, "call me Wally."

"And this is Leslie's roommate from California," Joyce resumed, "Ruth Burns."

Ruth took Wally's outstretched hand.

I cringed.

California? Oh, great — they probably think they're hot stuff.

"We picked up Ruth in Quito," Joyce continued. "She'll be staying with us for a few days."

Joyce looked at me.

"Oh, I'm sorry," said Wally as he remembered that I was standing behind him. "This is Kevin Kerrigan, a medical student from Florida." Handshakes were exchanged all around.

Joyce forged ahead, "Leslie and Ruth are both nurses and are interested in missions. Do you have time to give them a quick tour of the hospital? Sorry for the short notice, but Dave wants us at the hangar by eight."

"Sure, no problem."

With that, Wally led off into the hospital, narrating as he went. I followed a short distance behind, observing. Admittedly, they were cute girls, but you could tell by the way they were dressed that they were spoiled rich kids. They were wearing gold jewelry – in the jungle, of all places. My worst fears were confirmed when the blonde started asking about what type of ventilators we used for patients who couldn't breathe on their own. She went into great detail describing the type of ventilators they used in the intensive care unit where she worked in southern California.

Gag me with a spoon. Typical American – this girl has no idea what we're dealing with here. I mean, this is the Amazon rain forest. We deal with life and death on a more primitive level than at your big-city, California hospital. We don't need any of your fancy MA-1 ventilators here.

To make matters worse, she kept making it abundantly clear that she was an ICU nurse. Nurses in the intensive care unit were among the most conceited people I had ever met. They delighted in trying to show off that they knew more than us medical students.

Why don't you just go back to California where you belong?

I didn't actually say any of that, of course, but I could have. In my heart, I knew I was right.

At the end of the whirlwind tour Wally conversed quietly with Joyce, while I tried my best to be friendly to the two stuck-up brats. I wasn't making much headway when Joyce suddenly exclaimed, "Uh-oh, it's eight o'clock. Come on, we have to hurry."

They were off in a flurry and none too soon as far as I was concerned.

Wally and I were on our way back to the nurses' station to begin rounds when he turned to me and said, "Well, good news. Joyce is traveling out to an Atshuar village called Kapawari this weekend and she's agreed to take you along. You'll fly out on Friday."

"That's great!" I knew Wally would come through for me.

I wondered if either of the California surfer chicks would be going along, but I didn't dare ask. It didn't matter. I wasn't going to let them ruin this adventure.

"What's Atshuar?" I asked

"They're a tribe related to the Shuar." Wally had a wistful look in his eye. "I've been to Kapawari," he began softly.

"Really? When?"

"About ten years ago. Frank Drown ... have you met him? He's a missionary in Makuma with Joyce."

"Frank Drown?" I was incredulous. "No, I haven't met him, but I read about him. Isn't he the one who led the expedition into Auca land to recover the bodies of the five missionaries? You know him?"

"Yes," he answered in an offhand manner. "Anyway, about ten years ago he asked me to canoe downriver with him and a chief named Tsantiacu. We were going to visit a group of Atshuar living down near the border with Peru. The Ecuadorian military stopped us near the border and wouldn't let us go any farther, so instead we headed back upriver on a small tributary to the village of Kapawari. It was an amazing experience. I think we were the first white men these people had ever seen."

Suddenly, this trip was beginning to get my interest.

"Really? What did you do there?"

"Well, we weren't there long," Wally admitted, "probably less than twenty-four hours. I took a look at some of the people who were sick and treated them the best I could. Tsantiacu and Frank shared the gospel with them, though I don't remember any of them actually responding."

Ignoring the last comment, I pressed, "So, what's it like? Is it really primitive there?"

"Oh yes, it's quite primitive," he began, his voice trailing off. He looked pensive.

"Is there something you're not telling me?"

The question seemed to bring Wally back from a faraway place.

"What? Uh, no. I was just thinking about Tsantiacu. He was one of the first converts among the Atshuar and had a big impact among his people." Wally had a sad expression on his face.

"Had?" I asked. "What happened?"

"That's what I was just thinking about. When we left Kapawari, we met up briefly with another Atshuar chief named Tariri. Tariri was an old enemy of Tsantiacu's and they had each killed many members of one another's families. Tsantiacu told Tariri of his new faith in Christ and of his desire to forgive and put the killings behind him. Before we left, they made arrangements to visit one another."

"And did they?"

"Yes, they did. But while Tsanticu, his son and his son-in-law were asleep in Tariri's hut, Tariri and his family murdered them."

"What?" I was incredulous. Before coming to Ecuador, I had never personally known any murder victim. But here, killing people seemed to be accepted as a normal part of life.

"Yeah, I'm afraid so. Then, to make matters worse, they shrank their enemies' heads to have as trophies. It kicked off a new round of revenge killings that ended up claiming more than a dozen lives. What a way to live," Wally ended by giving voice to my thoughts.

Strangely, this new information, rather than causing me to have second thoughts about this trip, made it all the more enticing. Now, Friday couldn't come fast enough.

Chapter 8
Leslie's Oblivion

I was vaguely aware of conversation going on around me. Carol Osterhus had been nice enough to invite us into her living room to wait while the weather cleared. Her husband Dave, Olie Olson's fellow MAF pilot, was preparing our flight. The Osterhus' home was a huge two-story wooden building with a porch surrounding three sides of it. It was still affectionately known as the Saint house, despite the fact that none of the Nate Saint family had lived there for more than a decade.

"Yep, hurry up and wait – that's the MAF motto," Carol joked.

She and Joyce shared news about mutual friends and occasionally offered explanations, or else asked Ruth and me questions to draw us into the conversation. Normally, I would have been very involved, but today I was not feeling normal. In fact, I did something that was totally uncharacteristic of me. I picked up an old magazine, sat calmly on the couch in front of the fireplace and began thumbing through it in hopes that it would discourage anyone from talking to me. I slowly turned the pages, shocked at the inner excitement I felt. My mind raced, carrying my emotions along as it replayed the sequence of events that had just occurred. When I realized what was happening, I scolded myself.

Leslie, snap out of it! Get hold of yourself.

But, try as I might, I couldn't get my thoughts to focus on the conversation around me or the magazine I was holding. I felt helpless as wave after wave of emotion swept over me. Absent-mindedly I turned the pages of the magazine I was holding, but the written words held no meaning for me. My thoughts kept drifting back to the hospital tour we had just taken.

What is that guy doing out here? He's so good looking! Is he interested in missions? Wouldn't that be wonderful if the Lord could bring a man into my life who shared the same love of the Indians and desire to serve the Lord that I did? – someone who loved jungle life and wanted to be here ministering to needy people. But – is he even a Christian? What was his name? Oh yeah, Kevin. I hope he didn't notice me glancing at him during the tour. I think maybe he was aware of me, too. It made me a bit self-conscious. But it's over now. Why can't I get him out of my mind? I don't suppose I'll ever see him again. I'm going back to the jungle and who knows what will happen to him?

I determined to banish Kevin from my thoughts by concentrating on Dale. Things were looking up in that area. Ruth set my mind at ease soon after her arrival in Quito. She assured me that there was nothing going on between Dale and her. Dale was still very much interested in me. Ruth was as puzzled as I was as to why I had not received any mail from him. She was almost certain he had written to me nearly every day since I left. Also, she told me that Dale was very excited about coming down to Ecuador himself. And so was I! It would be so nice to see him again. My mind wandered ...

I felt like such an idiot trying to relate my high tech, specialized nursing experience with the rustic form of medicine they were practicing. But both Kevin and Dr. Swanson were so kind not to make me feel stupid. At one point during the tour – in the tiny pharmacy, I think – I asked a question. Kevin volunteered the answer and, as our eyes met, I felt like he was looking right through me! I had to avert my gaze. I was afraid that if I continued looking at him, he would surely realize I was attracted to him.

Attracted to him? I didn't even know anything about him.

They said he was a medical student. That could be good or bad. The good was that he would have some medical knowledge that I could respect, unlike one of my previous boyfriends who was always into the latest wacky health food fad. On the other hand, it probably meant he was only interested in money and status like all the other doctors I knew.

I remembered what a huge disappointment that had been for me when I began working at the hospital. You would think that working in a teaching hospital would be a perfect set-up – all those eligible young doctors and medical students. But my early hopes were soon dashed as I talked to the interns and residents who rotated through the ICU. A lot of them were cute and some of them were pretty nice, but they all seemed so shallow. I prided myself on not being superficial, on bypassing the social niceties of small talk and getting right down to heart issues. I think some people found it intimidating, but I always felt like "Why waste time talking about things that don't really matter?" One of the questions I would ask each of the doctors was why they had decided to go into medicine. I was shocked by their answers. It seemed that almost every one said, "To make lots of money", or some variation of that theme. And the way they said it indicated that it should have been totally obvious, like what other possible answer could there be? I had expected at least some of them to say that it was because they wanted to help their fellow man, or to alleviate suffering, or something like that, but they were all the same. Why should I think this guy would be any different than all the rest?

But, if Kevin was only interested in money, what was he doing out here?

My thoughts were like a runaway train now. I had no control over them. Silently, I calculated.

If he's still in medical school, it could mean that he's younger than me. But they say you should marry a man a few years younger than you anyway, since women tend to live longer. Marry? What am I talking about?

I was shocked at what I was thinking. After all, I had promised myself I would never even date, let alone consider marrying, a doctor.

It was more than just the money thing. They were all obsessed with sex. Crass jokes and sexual innuendos seemed to be a part of the culture of hospital life, especially in the ICU. It just made me sick.

I remember one of the doctors asking me out for dinner. He was a handsome guy and popular with all the nurses, so I think he expected me to feel honored. And maybe I would have been except for one little detail – he was married. When I pointed this out to him in declining his offer, he scoffed at the idea and tried to belittle me.

"Oh, so you're too good to go out with me, huh? And here I had heard you were a Christian," he said in mock surprise.

"I am."

"Really? And I thought Christians were supposed to love everybody. You're not being very loving to me now, are you?"

Right then and there I decided I would never, ever marry a doctor. They were the most shallow people I had ever known. Here they were, some of the most intelligent and capable people on the face of the earth, but they were only interested in using the talents God had given them for their own benefit. It was so disappointing.

There was no reason to think this guy would be any different from the rest.

Besides, I prided myself on not being boy-crazy like some of my girlfriends were. I wasn't about to go chasing after him. He was living in Shell and I was in Makuma, and that was the end of that.

Still, wouldn't it be wonderful if God provided a man with the same heart as mine to serve Him overseas?

"Leslie, hello-o. Leslie? Earth to Leslie. Come in, please."

I looked up to see my three companions staring at me. I was so embarrassed.

"That must be a fascinating article you're reading."

I slammed the magazine closed and set it down.

"Feel free to take it with you," Carol offered. "You can send it back with Dave next week when he flies you out to Kapawari."

"Oh, that reminds me," said Joyce. "I talked to Wally, and that medical student we just met will be coming with us."

My heart leapt.

"I have to admit," she continued, "I'm a little uncomfortable having a man come with the two of us. I've never done anything like this before. I don't know why I agreed to it. Oh well. I'll radio Kapawari and have them make proper arrangements to house the three of us. Anyway, he seemed like a very nice young man, don't you think?"

I stared at her, unable to say a word. I felt like something had me by the throat, keeping me from forming sounds. Thankfully, Joyce didn't seem to notice. She went on.

"Apparently, he's pretty quiet. But they say he's jumped in with both feet and has been a real asset at the hospital. Anyway, I guess we'll get a chance to find out about him for ourselves. Should be interesting."

Interesting? Interesting? Try terrifying!

My thoughts raced ahead to the coming week. To be honest, I don't really remember much about Ruth's visit.

Chapter 9
Kevin's Quest

"Libre," Dave Osterhus shouted out the open window of the small plane to no one in particular. The engine coughed to life as he turned the ignition. The single propeller seemed to reverse direction for an instant before it became a blur. We inched forward out of the open hangar and onto the wide concrete driveway. Dave applied the brakes as he craned his neck to see through my side of the canted windshield. Standing on a berm between the driveway and a narrow gravel road was Dave's young son, Danny. Danny stood on tiptoes to peer down the road descending to our left. Satisfied, he glanced over his right shoulder in the opposite direction and then frantically waved us on. Dave wasted no time in crossing the road and taxiing to our end of the grass airstrip. He turned the nose of the plane to face in the direction of the mountains and waited with engine idling. After a brief interchange in Spanish through his headset radio, he gunned the engines and we were off.

As the Cessna 180 lifted off the runway, my anticipation soared to new heights and my imagination ran wild. The oppressive weight of the humid jungle air was not enough to keep the small plane from climbing, any more than it was enough to dampen my excitement. The tiny outpost of Shell grew ever smaller as we ascended in an arc above it. Dave adjusted our setting to a south by southeast heading. Our destination was the Atshuar village of Kapawari, deep in the Amazon rain forest. As I turned to get a final view of Shell, I caught a glimpse of the conical peak of Sangay in the distance.

An active volcano, Sangay was one of a dozen snow-capped Andean mountains that bisected the nation of Ecuador from north to south. The closest of these peaks, Tunguragua, although only 35 miles west of Shell, was characteristically shrouded in mist as was its even taller, jagged neighbor, El Altar. In all probability Sangay, too, would soon be clouded over as the warming, humid air of the rain forest rose to meet the artic chill of the majestic Andes.

Within minutes, the view beneath us spread out in all directions as far as the eye could see. The textured dark green carpet was broken only by the numerous tributaries emptying their *café-au-lait* cargo of eroded mountain soil into the Pastaza River, itself a headwater of the mighty Amazon. I wondered how long it would take for the Andean soil to be deposited at the river's mouth three thousand miles away in Brazil. The continuous drone of the plane's engine prevented any normal conversation. Dave pointed out the occasional clearing in the vegetation representing *chacras* – subsistence farms hacked out of the ever-encroaching rain forest.

As we continued our course south of the Pastaza River into Morona-Santiago province, the occasional bright reflection from corrugated tin gave way to palm-thatched roofs. Had we been traveling our route by foot we would have also noticed a gradual shift in language from Quechua to Shuar. The Shuar, as well as their much less numerous neighbors to the north, the Waodani, are the original inhabitants of the rain forest. The proud, warrior ancestors of both tribes had fended off incursions by the Incans as well as the Spanish conquerors of the Incan empire. Now, however, there were other forces at play which made the Shuar and Waodani lands an irresistible prize. Large deposits of oil beneath their ancestral lands set these tribal people irrevocably on a collision course with modern day conquerors.

That thought caused me to ponder what I was hoping to gain by invading the remote peacefulness enjoyed by these people.

Was I, too, on some ephemeral treasure hunt? Was I seeking the utopia of a simpler, more innocent way of life? Or was my search for something deeper still? Perhaps I was looking for meaning in life. Could I possibly discover such a hidden treasure in a remote jungle village populated by primitive people using prehistoric means to scratch a living from the mysterious rain forest? Only time would tell.

The Shuar, formerly known as Jivaros, and their Atshuar cousins are infamous as the inventors of the still-secret process by which the heads of their enemies are shrunken to the size of a fist – reason enough for my excitement and anticipation. I was being given the opportunity to drop out of the sky into a stone-age civilization where men still hunted monkeys and birds in the forest canopy, using poison-tipped darts shot from eight foot long blowguns. But, first, we had another stop to make to pick up a couple of companions. After twenty minutes of flying, the jungle clearing of Makuma came into view and we prepared to land.

With great skill earned by years of jungle flying, Dave touched the Cessna down and bumped along the grassy airstrip. Out my side window I caught a glimpse of the passengers we had come to pick up. Two women were standing along the edge of the strip with several gym bags and woven wicker baskets at their feet. Surrounding them were a half dozen or so Indians whose short stature, bronzed complexion and long, straight, black hair distinguished them from our awaiting passengers. Joyce offered the more striking contrast. She was a tall woman even by U. S. standards, standing six feet tall. Her head, topped with curly, light brown hair, towered well above any of the Indians around her. As always, her face was lit up in a smile as she waved at us. I strained to see who was with her. At her side was a slender woman with long, straight blond hair which was highlighted all the more by her olive skin. The shapeless knee-length shift and rubber galoshes could not conceal Leslie's athletic figure.

Dave swung the tail-dragger in a 180-degree turn near the end of the airstrip and headed toward the waiting group at midfield. The crowd restrained itself until he killed the engine. They then approached the plane *en masse*. Dave hopped out, greeted Joyce and Leslie, and spoke with a couple of the Shuar men briefly. I waited in my seat, unsure of proper etiquette in this situation. Should I get out in order to help, or would that be some sort of safety violation? In less than a minute, Dave loaded the women's gear behind the rear seats, then helped them aboard and strapped them in.

"Where's Ruth?" I asked.

"She's still up at the house, packing. Dave will stop back by here to pick up her and the Haynes brothers and take them as far as Latacunga." Joyce said, as though I should know who the Haynes brothers were. "They'll catch a taxi or bus the rest of the way to Quito. She leaves for the U. S. tomorrow."

"How was her time here?"

I was careful not to direct the question to either one of them directly, thinking Leslie would naturally answer an inquiry about her roommate. But she just sat there.

"She had a little trouble handling all the mud on the trails," Joyce finally answered, "but overall I think she had a good time."

The Shuar backed away from the plane, waving as Dave swung back up into his seat. In no time we were airborne again.

"Full schedule today," Dave yelled above the roar of the engine as we gained altitude.

I knew our destination was quite a distance – nearly to the border with Peru. Once again, the constant hum of the engine precluded any meaningful conversation. That, however, didn't seem to dissuade the passengers in the rear of the cabin, who persisted in shouting to one another. Sporadically Joyce would point out what, to her, were recognizable landmarks in the seemingly trackless forest below. I found myself turning at every opportunity to catch a glimpse of Leslie, seated behind Dave. I couldn't keep my eyes off of her. It was as though I had never seen a woman before.

Whoa, Kevin, you've been living in the jungle too long. Don't forget how she acted in the hospital.

That recent memory helped subdue my passion. I forced myself to look out the window at the featureless jungle below. The occasional village clearing became less and less frequent the farther into the forest we flew.

Were the answers I was searching for down there somewhere?

Chapter 10
Leslie's Remoteness

"Kapawari International Airport", Dave announced.

He pointed out a speck in the jungle made up of a tiny airstrip lined by a half dozen thatch-roofed huts. The plane banked sharply. Dave passed over the village to be certain the landing strip was clear of people, animals or debris. He made a sweeping turn over the treetops, faced the Cessna into the wind and laid it down on the grass with hardly a shudder.

MAF flight landing at Kapawari

I was glad to have the flight over with. It had not been as enjoyable as previous flights I had taken. I spent the entire trip trying my best to ignore Kevin. I was proud of myself for how successful I had been at accomplishing my task, but it was tiring. A couple of times I thought I caught him staring at me, but I couldn't be sure. I had taken care to choose my favorite red-and-white-checked dress for the occasion. I tend to look better in bright colors, although it's hard to look good in black tights and rubber galoshes.

Oh well, who cares?

I noticed on our approach that there was no one waiting for us and wondered what that meant. But by the time Dave brought the plane to a halt, a dozen people – mostly women and children – were running from the forest onto the airstrip and up to the plane. Only one man was in the crowd. He was a lean, muscular fellow with the fine features and clear complexion that distinguishes the Shuar from the ruddy, mountain Quechuas. He took the lead in approaching the plane and broke into a broad grin upon recognizing Joyce through the rear window.

"*Pujamek,*" he called out as Joyce deftly maneuvered her frame through the tiny door of the Cessna.

"*Eeh, pujajai,*" she answered, extending her hand in a hearty greeting.

With that, the entire welcoming committee broke out together into a jabbering chorus. Kevin came over and stood close to my side.

"Do you understand any of what they're saying?" he asked. "Are they speaking Shuar?"

"No, it's Atshuar, but it's close enough to Shuar that they understand one another. I'm afraid I'm lost, though," I admitted.

For reasons that I can't explain, I felt pleased at his question and the interest he was showing in me.

"I can greet someone in Shuar, count to ten, say 'yes' or 'no', things like that. But when they get going like this, I'm lost."

114

"Well, then, I guess it's you and me this weekend," he said with a sly wink.

I should have been offended by the presumption of his comment, but instead I felt the beginning of a bond with him. His quiet, gentle voice lent an intimate air to our brief conversation. The two of us followed Joyce's lead and went about shaking everyone's hand. Stealing glances across the short distance that separated us, I began to study this young man. He was dressed in a faded navy blue polo shirt, Levis and well-worn tennis shoes. I noticed he made eye contact with the people as he smiled and shook their hands. He had such sincere, clear blue eyes.

Across the crowd, Joyce shouted something to Dave, who nodded in agreement. One of the Atshuar children was sent away and returned a minute later with a hand-woven basket. Inside were two live chickens sitting calmly, their feet tightly bound together. Dave secured the basket in the rear of the plane. We thanked Dave and bid him good-bye, agreeing to be ready when he returned early Monday. Dave shooed everyone away from the plane and, just like that, he was gone.

"Well, I guess there's no turning back now," Kevin observed.

I wondered whether he was feeling any regrets.

With silence having returned to the village, Joyce made the introductions. "Hey, guys. I want you to meet a dear friend of mine," she began in English to Kevin and me. Turning, she then continued in Spanish, "*Quiero presentarles a un buen amigo mio,* Ernesto Vargas," indicating the man who had first greeted her upon arrival.

Ernesto offered his hand. "*Mucho gusto,*" he intoned.

"*Igualmente,*" I responded, pleased that I had been able to come up with an appropriate answer.

From there the conversation returned to Shuar, a language with which Ernesto was clearly more comfortable. I was envious of the way Joyce could skip from one language to another.

Curious, at a break in the conversation, Kevin pulled Joyce to one side. "Ernesto isn't a very Shuar-sounding name. Who is he?"

"Oh, he's Shuar all right," answered Joyce, "but he's not from here. He lives in Pitkirishka, a Shuar community closer to Shell. For some reason, the Shuar there take on more Spanish-sounding names."

I noted a hint of disappointment in her voice. I knew why. It upset Joyce that the Shuar felt the need to become more like the majority of Ecuador's population, loosing some of their identity in the process. Any displeasure she was feeling didn't last long.

"Ernesto is a wonderful Christian man. He's been here for a couple of days already, teaching."

We were escorted to our accommodations, a thatch-roofed hut just at the edge of the airstrip. It was elevated three or four feet off the ground on pilings. The doorless entryway was approached by way of a palm tree trunk laid diagonally. Rough steps were hewn into the log. The walls and floor of the hut were made of chonta wood slats. There was a common room as you entered with two smaller rooms on either side toward the rear. The interior walls were also constructed of split chonta wood. Joyce and I were offered one of the rear rooms and Kevin the other. The only furnishing in our living space was a split bamboo platform for sleeping, raised a couple of feet off the floor. It took a few moments for my eyes to adjust from the bright sunlight outside. Once they did, I could see a number of dark eyes peering through the many slits in the exterior walls. It came as no shock. I had grown used to it. Privacy was not a major consideration in the Shuar value system. As always, the people were very curious about these large, pale strangers who had invaded their world. The kids were particularly curious, but at the same time guarded, often hiding shyly behind their parents or older siblings.

We weren't given much time to get settled. Almost as soon as we set down our bags, a man started calling to Joyce from outside.

"Come on, Les, he wants us to be on his team for volleyball."

I knew Ecuadorians played with only three-man teams.

"But what about Kevin? I'll let him play in my place."

I heard Kevin's voice from the other side of the interior wall.

"Oh, no you don't. You're not getting out of it that easily. You play. I'll watch. This should be good."

As the three of us descended the log steps into the bright sunlight again, I was amazed at how many more Atshuar had silently appeared from the surrounding rain forest. And now the accumulating crowd contained a lot more men.

Behind our hut was another structure which was more of a shelter than a building. There was the same thatched roof, but the split bamboo walls only went halfway up. Many of the Atshuar women began congregating there. In the center of the dirt floor was a pile of ash with a couple of large logs protruding. Within a few short minutes the women transformed the ash heap into a blazing fire. Over the flames they suspended an iron cooking pot filled with water. As the shelter filled with smoke from the damp wood, I recognized the familiar pungent odor that permeates the Shuar people and everything they own.

Atshuar women preparing yuca and platano

There was a clearing between our hut and this outdoor kitchen. This was where the makeshift volleyball court was located. With little fanfare, the game was begun. Joyce's height was a distinct advantage. A murmur of appreciation arose from the crowd whenever she reached to get what seemed to be an impossible shot. I, on the other hand, was finding it difficult to adjust to the game. The ball they used was much harder than any volleyball I had ever played with and hurt my hands each time I hit it. But the real barrier to my ability to play well was my outfit. The red and white dress I had chosen earlier that day was the shortest one I had brought with me from the U. S. Each time I went up for a shot my skirt rode up my thigh. I felt self-conscious. Fortunately, I had tights on, but even so I wasn't sure if that was culturally acceptable to the Atshuar. And, besides that, Kevin was watching. I was very aware of his presence, even though I pretended to be involved in the game. After each shot or jump that I made, I grabbed my skirt and tugged it down as low as I could. I didn't want to appear immodest and I certainly didn't want him to be attracted to me for the wrong reasons. I was just about ready to quit and insist that Kevin take my place when he got called away.

Chapter 11
Kevin's Clumsiness

I hated to leave. I was enjoying myself immensely, watching Leslie play volleyball. It was obvious she had natural athletic ability. And she was not afraid to get dirty. But what I admired most was the shapeliness of her long legs, despite being hidden by those hideous black tights.

Abruptly, my role as an interested but passive member of the audience came to an end. As more and more young men and boys arrived from all directions in the forest, a game of soccer took form on the air strip. The Atshuar men invited me to join them. It seemed to come more in the form of a demand than a request. Soccer was a game with which I was only mildly acquainted. I soon proved that fact, much to the delight of the other players. They laughed uproariously as more than once I took a mighty swing with my leg at the ball only to miss it completely. On one such occasion I landed flat on my back. It was a rather humbling experience, especially since I took pride in my athletic achievements. After all, I had been captain of the football and wrestling teams in my high school. As an undergraduate at Notre Dame I had been a three-time welterweight boxing champ. That was small consolation, however, as I picked myself up from the ground. Much to my chagrin, there was Leslie, watching the whole sorry episode. I was tempted to go over and explain to her what a good athlete I really was and how this was just not my game. In that instant she was called to join Joyce and the other women at the cooking fire.

She probably wouldn't believe me anyway. Who could blame her. She must think I'm a real loser. Oh well, what do I care what she thinks.

Mercifully, the game ended before I threw up from being so out of shape. I followed the other players to a small clearing near the cooking hut. In the middle of the clearing was the stump of a tree which had been cut off about waist high. A hole, the size of my two fists, had been bored through it. The men placed a long pole through this opening and then stuffed pieces of cut sugar cane alongside the pole in the space that remained. Using the pole as a lever, they squeezed juice out of the cane, catching it in a wooden bowl. This they offered to me before passing it around to everyone else. It made for a cool and refreshing drink.

Using cane press to make cool drink after the soccer game

By this time we were all ready to eat. We gathered in the cooking hut and, after Joyce said the blessing in Shuar, the women handed each of the men a large banana leaf which served as a plate. On each leaf were a piece of fish and one or two large pieces of boiled *yuca*, a tuber that was one of the few crops that grew well in the rain forest. The fish was very good. The *yuca* was not unlike a potato, though more starchy, dry and practically tasteless. Fortunately, Joyce had brought along a little package of salt. After a few bites, I felt like I needed something to wash it down with. I was offered a drink made from mashed-up bananas. The drink itself was sort of semi-solid, so did little to help the *yuca* go down.

Joyce just laughed, "Count your blessings -- at least its not *chicha*."

"What's that?" I asked.

"*Chicha* is another drink that the Shuar make," she answered. "It's made by the women. They sit around a pot chewing *yuca*, then spit it into the pot and let it ferment. It's a real favorite."

"I'll bet. Have you ever had any?"

"Oh yes, often, although the Shuar have learned to serve me only the non-alcoholic variety, which isn't allowed to ferment as long."

"Have you ever been offered anything you just couldn't eat?"

"Well, just like for most of us, it's pretty offensive to the Shuar if you refuse something they offer you to eat or drink. I always try to eat whatever I'm offered, but I must admit there is one delicacy I've never been able to acquire a taste for. The Shuar love to dig these big, fat, greasy beetle larva called grub worms out of rotting logs and pop them in their mouths like peanuts. They just shake their heads when I turn down their offers. They can't understand how I can resist such a delicacy. They're probably secretly happy, since it means more for them."

When the meal was ended, Joyce asked in a cheerful voice, "Well, are you ready to start seeing patients? I noticed one of the little girls has pus in her eyes. Let's see if we can find her."

With that, I grabbed the box of medicines and other supplies I had brought from the hospital. We made our way to the far end of the airstrip where the meeting house was located. This structure shared many of the construction features of the home we were staying in but was much larger, with rounded ends. The roof was supported by large vertical palm trunks creating an ample open space inside. This building rested on the ground and rough wooden benches were arranged haphazardly around the bare dirt floor. The gaggle of villagers had followed us into the building. Joyce spoke to them, and soon a number of them slipped away while the remainder pushed a small, shy girl to the front of the crowd. Joyce spoke to her gently while gesturing toward me. Soon, one after another in the crowd began to offer their opinion and suggestions and in no time Joyce was lost in conversation, punctuated often by peals of laughter.

That left me alone at the edge of the crowd with the shy little girl. She was a beautiful girl of perhaps five or six years of age. She wore a faded, threadbare dress and, like everyone else in the village, was barefoot. Her otherwise attractive facial features were marred by the yellow crust lining her soft brown eyes.

Kevin sees his first patient at the "clinic" in Kapawari

I busied myself emptying the box of medicines and arranging them on a bench in front of me, occasionally stealing a glance her way. She watched me intently from a distance. Not knowing what else to do, I began talking to her in English.

"Hi. That's a pretty dress you have on. Did your mommy make it for you? How old are you?"

As I spoke, I inched down the bench in her direction. She held her ground. As I approached, I reached out and patted her on the head.

"My, what big eyes you have. But it looks like there's something in them. Can I take a look?"

Without moving or making a sound, she allowed me to examine her red and swollen conjunctiva.

"I think I have just the thing for you."

I reached for a tube of antibiotic eye ointment, wondering how I was going to hold the girl and apply the ointment at the same time. I looked up to see Leslie standing a short distance away, observing the unfolding scene.

Chapter 13
Leslie's Fantasy

My eyes were fixed upon them, but my mind was far, far away.

Wouldn't it be wonderful if God would provide me with a man who had the same heart for these people that I do? I wonder if He would do that for me.

I felt a mix of hope and shame – shame for what, or rather who, had brought these thoughts to mind. As I watched Kevin approach the little girl, I admired his compassion. Her unkempt body and filthy clothes did not deter him from treating her with the same consideration any doctor would give to a rich little girl in the U. S. He seemed to recognize the value of every person – rich or poor, great or small – made in God's image. You would think that anyone who had volunteered their time to come to treat the Shuar would be the same, but I had seen other doctors come to the jungle to offer medical care who, it seemed to me, had other motives. They talked to the Shuar as though they considered them lesser beings. Sometimes they would treat them as curiosities, lining them up for staged photos, insisting they wear "authentic" Indian outfits. Usually, the Shuar complied, but it pained me to see it. I detected none of that in the way Kevin interacted with this shy little girl. I couldn't help but feel a bond with him as I realized that he shared by love and compassion for people. All of that was good, of course, but there was a problem.

On our flight back to Makuma from Shell, after our tour of the hospital, Joyce just couldn't stop talking about what a nice young man that medical student was. But then she dropped the bombshell.

"Wally said they are not sure if he is a believer. Sara Risser told Wally that he was from a Catholic background, but she didn't really know where he stood with the Lord."

My heart sank at the news. I had girlfriends who did "missionary dating" in hopes of winning some guy to the Lord. I was definitely not interested in that. I figured, even if it worked and the guy became a believer, there would be such a difference in spiritual maturity that the girl would end up being the leader in the relationship. That was not what I wanted. And now here I was, feeling my heart drawn to this guy whom I didn't really know, and daydreaming about a future with him.

"Could I get a little help here?" It was Kevin.

"What? Oh, sure. I'm sorry. Of course, let me help."

Between the two of us we managed to get a thin stream of ointment in both of the girl's eyes. She offered no resistance. I found that amazing considering the fact that two aliens who had just invaded her world were squirting a strange substance into her inflamed and tender eyes. As we finished I became aware that the noisy conversation in the meeting house had ceased. I looked up to see the crowd's attention riveted on us. Several of the older women were nodding their heads and Joyce was beaming from ear to ear.

"Well, Kevin, you've made a hit with the Atshuar."

"What do you mean?" he asked. "I haven't done anything yet."

"You may not think so, but they do. The Shuar and Atshuar are skeptical of medicines taken by mouth for any ailment other than intestinal problems. After all, what good does it do to put medicine in your stomach if the problem is in your leg, for instance?"

"Makes sense," he agreed.

"They think it's much better to get an injection, preferably as near the site of the illness as possible. But the best, of course, is to apply strong medicine directly on the problem – like you've done."

There was a low murmuring among the audience and further consultation with Joyce, followed by more nods among the Atshuar women. As if with one voice they exclaimed, "*Eeh. Doctor Tivi.*"

"What's that all about?" Kevin asked.

"Well, the women wanted to know your name. Our names are hard for them to pronounce, so we take on Shuar names. Mine is Puench. And now yours is *Doctor Tivi*".

"Wow, sounds impressive," I mocked. "**Doctor** Tivi, I presume?"

Kevin acted as though he was embarrassed, but I suspected he was secretly pleased.

He said, "And what about you? Do you have a Shuar name?"

"I'm Maswink," I said as I held my head high.

"Ma's wink?" he repeated, making a great show of opening his mouth and tilting his head in my direction, while mimicking an exaggerated wink. "What kind of name is that?"

He laughed.

I was hurt, stung. He was making fun of me.

"It's Shuar," I said, turning back to the little girl still standing there.

I think he realized he had crossed some boundary. Trying to make amends, he said in a cheerful tone, "Well, Maswink, we've got a lot of work ahead of us here".

More Atshuar had begun queuing up to see Doctor Tivi. As we worked together, trying our best to understand what concerns the patients had, I couldn't help but feel that Kevin was being very attentive to me. I was certainly aware of him. But I didn't know if he was only trying to make up for having hurt my feelings about my Shuar name, or if he was genuinely interested in me. Regardless of the motivation, I enjoyed it.

The line of waiting patients dwindled as the afternoon drew to a close. Joyce rejoined us and began to prepare for the Bible lesson she was to give that evening. Joyce was often invited to Shuar and, sometimes, Atshuar villages to teach the Bible. This presented a dilemma in that it was the men who took leadership among the indigenous people. That was the reason Joyce had invited Ernesto to join her this weekend. Kevin and I helped set up the meeting place, then we all sat outside waiting for the Atshuar to arrive. Soon there appeared a beautiful sunset over the rain forest on the other side of the airstrip. The sky looked as though it were on fire. Dark lavender clouds were sandwiched between lower layers of bright red and orange just above the forested horizon and deep purple skies above, fading into a cobalt blue canopy.

"What a life," Kevin said. "These people have nothing, yet they are so happy and carefree. Life is so much simpler here. Now I know what people mean when they talk about 'the innocent savage'."

Joyce said nothing, lost in contemplation at the fading sunset. I was disappointed at his comment and considered pointing out to him how naïve it was, but decided it was probably better to follow Joyce's example and let it pass.

In the waning light of dusk the entire population of Kapawari congregated at the meeting house. We were all packed side by side on the little wooden benches. Ernesto led us in several Shuar songs. Dr. Tivi and I found a Shuar hymnal that we shared and tried our best to sing along with everyone else.

Ernesto Vargas leading singing at the Bible conference

I was so encouraged. Kevin didn't seem at all hostile or even reluctant to participate. Perhaps I had misjudged his spiritual state. What's more, he seemed to be standing much closer to me than he had to, even considering the crowded conditions. My pulse raced as I sensed the warmth and strength of his body next to mine.

Soon Joyce was introduced and taught a Bible lesson complete with illustrations drawn on a flip chart she had brought along. I couldn't understand a word of what she was saying, but I sat there quietly so as not to distract those seated around me who were following every word. One illustration in particular seemed to strike a chord with the audience. Joyce drew a chasm like a steep river bank with a simple figure of a man on one side and a representation of God on the other. It was obvious from her tone of voice that the man really wanted to cross the river but could not find a way. The people were very sympathetic and visibly saddened as each attempt the man made ended in failure. Finally, Joyce drew a cross whose arms touched each bank, and the man happily walked across to the other side, much to the relief of the congregation.

Following the session we returned to our rooms. A number of the participants in the conference followed, each anxious to talk to Joyce in turn. Sensing these were private counseling sessions, and having heard our fill of Shuar for one day, Kevin and I inched our way just outside the hut. A warm breeze engulfed the night with the sweet scent of tropical vegetation. The expanse of the air strip was illuminated by a pale half-moon.

"So, were you able to catch much of Joyce's lesson?" I asked.

"Not a word," he admitted. "How about you?"

"I'm afraid not. I'm terrible at languages. There's a Shuar girl in Makuma named Chiki. She's really sweet and we get along well, but it's so hard not being able to talk with her. We wash dishes together and we're always laughing together about something or other. This summer I've been helping Joyce by sewing curtains and school clothes for her daughter Ruthie and..."

"I didn't know Joyce had a daughter," Kevin interrupted.

"Oh, really? Yeah, she has three kids. Anyway, I've been trying to teach Chiki how to use a treadle sewing machine. This is the second summer I've been with Joyce and, still, about all I can do is greet people. It's frustrating."

"So you've been here before? When was that?"

"Three years ago," I began, "with Joyce and her husband, John."

"Her husband? Where is he?"

"He died of cancer."

Kevin's face fell. "Oh, I'm sorry."

"Yeah, it was pretty rough on Joyce and the kids. Don was only 9 years old at the time, Bob, 8, and Ruthie, 6."

"That's sad. So you mean that Joyce and the kids moved back down here to the jungle alone?"

"Hm-hm, three months after John died. In fact, Joyce invited me to come back down last summer – she even sent me money to help with the airfare, would you believe – but I had just graduated and wanted to take state boards and get some nursing experience first. But, now I'm back. I've been having a great time with her and the kids this summer. Joyce is so much fun. She's always game for any new adventure. Like she says, people in the U. S. think, 'Oh, the poor, suffering missionaries' but here we are, living all the adventures they only get to watch on TV."

"I know what you mean. I could easily see myself living down here the rest of my life."

"Really?"

I tried not to over-react to what he said, but his statement stirred something deep within me. I think it was a renewed sense of hope about the future. During my years at Biola, I was always on the lookout for a man who shared my passion for missions. But it seemed that any guy interested in missions was, well frankly, kind of quirky. And the guys that I found attractive just weren't interested in missions. Now here was a guy who matched my idea of what a man should be and still seemed to share my enthusiasm for reaching out to people in other cultures. I was definitely attracted to him and anxious to explore the possibilities, but before I could pursue the conversation, Joyce poked her head through the doorway.

"Hey, they're all gone now. Anybody want a chocolate chip cookie?"

Whenever we traveled to outstations, Joyce brought a stash of homemade treats to supplement the bland diet provided by the Shuar. This particular batch I had made prior to our leaving Makuma. Soon the three of us were laughing and talking as we devoured the smuggled cookies. A single candle provided the only light. Its reflection in Kevin's eyes produced a magical effect.

As we went to our separate sides of the sleeping quarters, I felt strangely comforted by Kevin's presence nearby. I even imagined it would be nice to snuggle in bed next to him. I chided myself for having such thoughts and rolled over to try to sleep. As I lay on my sleeping bag atop the split bamboo platform in the dark, I could hear something flying around in the space above.

Soon, Kevin called out, "Hey, something just landed on me!"

"Bats." Joyce replied matter-of-factly.

"Vampire bats?"

"I don't think so. They're probably just fruit bats."

"You don't **think** so?" Kevin said. "That does it. I'm sleeping under this platform, not on top of it."

I fumbled for my camera in the darkness. Finding it in my bag, I pointed it in the direction of the next flapping sound and pushed the button. I thought I caught a glimps of the bat through the lens when the flash went off. I had to smile as I pulled my sleeping bag up over my head. I had spent the night in enough villages to be used to the bats, though I still cringed at the thought of their ugly faces flying toward me in the pitch dark. But it struck me as humorous the thought of this big, manly guy hiding beneath his bed. I lay awake thinking, dreaming.

What would tomorrow bring?

Chapter 15
Kevin's Humiliation

The next two days were marked by morning and evening Bible teaching sessions, following the same basic pattern that was initiated the night before. Although it got a little old not understanding what was being said, I tolerated the situation by convincing myself that something good and worthwhile was occurring in these people's lives, whether I understood it or not. Besides, it was a good excuse to get close to Leslie.

Leslie and I continued to see a variable number of patients following the teaching sessions. However, that still left plenty of free time which the Atshuar were all too happy to help us fill. The first morning, several of the men and boys brought out their blow guns to demonstrate. These weapons were a marvel of craftsmanship. Each stood eight feet long and ramrod straight. The shafts were pitch black, but at one end was attached a white mouthpiece made from the hollowed out leg bone of a wild boar. Peering through it gave one an unobstructed view as straight and true as any rifle barrel. With Joyce's help, I asked how in the world they were able to bore such a long straight barrel without any modern tools. They explained that they search for a long, straight pole of *chonta* palm. After rounding and smoothing the exterior surface, they split the pole down its length. Upon carefully cutting a notch down the exact middle of both halves, they bind the two halves together again by tightly wrapping lengths of wicker around the outside. The wicker is held in place and reinforced by application of a black, gummy resin that is allowed to dry and harden. Then long vines attached to sharp rocks of gradually increasing diameter are pulled back and forth through the length of the barrel until the desired caliber is attained.

The other indispensable item for hunting is the quiver of darts. The simple but elegant quiver is constructed from an appropriate length of bamboo shoot to include one of its horizontal dividers, positioned so as to constitute the floor of the quiver. Tightly bound to the quiver by lengths of wicker is a gourd, filled with kapok fiber that can be plucked through a hole in the gourd. The darts themselves are about the diameter of a toothpick down their entire nine-inch length. One end is finely sharpened, and its tip is covered with curare, a poison that the Shuar and Atshuar obtain from a plant growing in the rain forest. Curare is the naturally-occurring form of a type of medicine used to paralyze patients during operations. In this case, the curare enters the prey from the painted black tip of the dart. When the monkey tries to remove the dart, the tip breaks off at the notch that the hunter has made an inch or two back on the shaft. Soon, the monkey is paralyzed and falls out of the treetops to the hunter waiting below.

In order to shoot the blowgun, cotton-like kapok fiber has to be applied to the shaft of the dart to act as wadding. The Atshuar men demonstrated this to us by pulling off a piece of the fiber from the gourd and twirling it about the shaft of the dart a couple of inches from the blunt end. Then they twirled it around in their mouths to moisten it and shape it with their tongues. It looked simple enough, but my first attempts looked more like a misused cotton swab than the sleek, symmetric and aerodynamic forms they had effortlessly created. The Atshuar got a great kick out of my ineptitude.

Leslie, who seemed to get the hang of making the proper wadding much better than I, asked, "Have you ever shot a blowgun before?"

I admitted that I had not.

"Don and Bob taught me how to do it," she continued cheerfully. "They each have a short blow gun. We use them to shoot moths climbing on the screen of the porch in Makuma. The darts would go right through the screen. It was fun."

Big deal, how hard could it be to hit a fist-sized moth?

Then I said aloud, "You know, marksmanship is in my blood. My father is a retired Marine and highly-decorated veteran of the Korean War. He took part in the famous battle of the Frozen Chosin."

"Really? What a coincidence. My dad is a retired Marine."

"Oh yeah? Well, my dad was a member of the Marine Corps pistol team and has a mantle full of trophies to prove it. Sometimes he let me go with him to the firing range. Believe me, I'm no stranger to target practice."

"Were you in the military yourself?"

"Not exactly," I answered. "I'm on a Navy scholarship for med school, so I'm considered a Reserve officer, but I don't actually do anything with them – yet."

What I didn't tell her was that I had previous combat experience, of a sort. During the fall of sophomore year in high school, my buddies Kevin Rainey and Kenny Van Train and I had developed a fascination with BB guns. We talked my brother Terry, five years my junior, into playing war games with us. We issued him a cool-looking, pump- action pistol which could possibly hit a target ten feet away, if aimed up at a forty-five degree angle. We, meanwhile, were armed with CO_2-powered repeating carbines. My comrades-in-arms and I took up well-fortified positions on the top of a wooded knoll between the end of our cul-de-sac and the B&O railroad tracks. Terry was ordered to attack our position. Without boasting, I can truthfully say that nearly every time I fired, I was rewarded by the sound of a pitiful yelp from Terry – the little cry-baby. What did he expect? War is hell.

"Enough of this nonsense," I announced. "Let's do some shooting".

The Atshuar obliged by setting up a two-inch wide palm branch twenty paces away. I feigned interest as they each vied to show me their own technique, unfailingly sticking the dart in the palm branch with each shot they attempted.

I could stand it no longer. I reached out and confiscated a weapon to my liking. Deftly I slid a dart through the pig bone mouthpiece. My fingers moved quickly so as to create an impression of confidence. I also hoped that no one would notice the sorry appearance of the misshapen wad of kapok sitting asymmetrically to one side of my dart. Lifting the blowgun to aim, I was surprised at how difficult it was to hold the eight- foot shaft steady in the horizontal position. The longer I took to carefully aim, the more my arms, and thus the blowgun, began to shake. I knew I had to get the shot off quickly. Taking as big a breath as my lungs would allow, I exhaled forcefully into the mouthpiece. The deformed dart barely cleared the end of the barrel before it floated to the ground. The response was immediate and resonant. Howls of laughter echoed through the forest. I turned crimson as, without looking, I could see that Maswink was enjoying the farce as much as anyone else. How humiliating. My life couldn't get any worse – or so I thought.

Undoubtedly hoping for another opportunity to entertain themselves at the expense of the *gringos,* the Atshuar men made a great show of offering a blowgun to Maswink. She tried to demur, but they insisted. Finally, she obliged them. Lifting the blowgun and firing without hesitation, she nailed the palm branch, dead center. As the stunned Atshuar nodded their heads approvingly, I looked around for a hole to crawl into.

Apparently, wounded pride translates easily across cultures. Puancher, one of our fellow marksmen, tried to make amends by offering to take Leslie and me hunting with him. We jumped at the chance.

"Just a second," I called. "I want to get my camera in case we see some wildlife."

We followed Puancher down a muddy trail leading from the clearing into the rain forest. It became progressively darker as the forest canopy thickened the farther we penetrated. Soon Leslie and I were panting and perspiring profusely trying to keep pace with Puancher as he moved stealthily through the jungle. I kept looking up, hoping to catch a glimpse of a toucan, macaw or monkey that I could capture on film, but the foliage was too thick to see anything. I was beginning to get bored when, all of a sudden, Puancher stopped. Leslie and I held still, trying to sense what had changed in our environment to capture his attention. To me it all looked and sounded exactly as it had for the past twenty minutes of walking. Puancher, though, kept turning his head from side to side while looking up with intense concentration. With one hand he reached for his quiver. He began fingering several little trinkets that looked like bits of bones or twigs, suspended from the quiver with twine. Without looking, he chose one, brought it up to his lips and began making a shrill chirping sound. Soon, I heard an identical sound in the canopy above, coming closer and closer. After several minutes of this back-and-forth exchange between hunter and hunted, a beautiful fluorescent-green bird came into view. Without making a sound or taking his eyes off his prey, Puancher choose a dart, applied the kapok wadding and slid it into his blowgun as if in a single motion. As Puancher lifted the blowgun to his lips, I saw that I was perfectly positioned to capture the entire dramatic scene on film, frozen in time forever. Puancher's chest expanded. The lens shutter clicked. The bird flew off. No one said a word, but it was obvious that the hunt had ended. Puancher turned on his heel and, without looking at me, headed back down the trail toward the village.

Chapter 16
Leslie's Snag

"Kevin, come look at this," I called.

Several of the Atshuar women had followed us into our hut. One of them found a magnifying mirror that Joyce had brought. The women were taking turns looking into the mirror. Seeing their reflections in the clear glass made them giggle. As always, each covered her mouth with her hand when she laughed.

Soon, Joyce was joking with them and, even though we didn't understand the words, Kevin and I joined in the fun and laughter.

"I never really thought about it," said Kevin, "but I guess living out here, there's not much chance to see your reflection. Maybe in the river, but that's kind of murky."

I agreed. "It's easy to forget and take things for granted. I remember when I first got to Makuma how amazed the people were that my glasses would change color when I went in the sun."

"Well," grinned Joyce, "we've got another opportunity to introduce the citizens of Kapawari to a modern miracle of technology."

Joyce slipped inside her sleeping quarters, reappearing with a duffle bag. From it she produced three complete fishing rods and reels. She handed out the parts and we began to assemble them. Joyce said something in Shuar to a boy standing nearby. He disappeared into the forest.

"So how do the Shuar catch fish?" Kevin asked as we worked.

"It's kind of neat," I answered. "They find a plant called *barbasco* that grows in the jungle, mash it up and squeeze the juice into a section of river. It paralyzes the fish and they pop to the surface of the water like corks. They have wicker traps set up downstream to collect the fish. Another group of Shuar downriver wades in and picks up any floating fish that don't get caught in the traps."

"That doesn't sound very fair," said Kevin. "Isn't that against the Geneva Convention or something, using chemical warfare on poor, unsuspecting fish?"

"That's why we're here, to show them a more humane way," Joyce said, tying a vicious-looking treble hook to her line. "Right, Leslie?"

Kevin laughed. "You two are warped."

About that time, the Atshuar boy re-appeared with a handful of the largest grasshoppers I have ever seen. Off we trudged across the airstrip with several curious Atshuar following. The section of the river nearest the village paralleled the airstrip and was separated from it by a narrow band of forest. Even this far down river from the Andes the brown water rushed and churned. Quite a few trees along the bank had fallen over into the river. We found a canoe lying on the bank that the Atshuar had hollowed out of a single log. In order to get a better shot at the river and avoid branches hanging overhead, we placed the canoe perpendicular to the current, wedging it between the steep bank and a partially submerged log. With the dugout secured, we marched out onto our makeshift fishing pier.

Joyce explaining the finer points of rod and reel to Atshuar men

We made a great show of it, Joyce explaining each step of the process in great detail to the crowd of Atshuar who had gathered on the bank to watch. The three of us agreed to coordinate our casts so as not to foul our lines. On the count of three, we all let fly. My aim was a bit high, causing my line to wrap itself around an overhanging branch like a well-hit tetherball. Kevin had better success, dropping his weighted line out near the middle of the river. Unfortunately, his bait came off and went flying in a different direction. The baited hook on Joyce's line got stuck in the back of her dress. The Atshuar clapped and howled at our antics. They proved to have a short attention span, however. By the time we had untangled and hauled in our lines, the Atshuar had grown bored and drifted off to their homes to fix dinner. The three of us each eventually got a baited hook out into the water. After a half hour without a nibble we skulked back to our hut.

By the time we arrived, the Atshuar had delivered a meal of cooked fish and *yuca*, leaving it wrapped in leaves on the floor of our hut.

Kevin laughed. "I'm glad somebody had better luck than us fishing."

Joyce turned to Kevin. "Would you say grace?" she asked. Her tone of voice was the same as if she had been asking how the weather was.

I was surprised by her boldness, not knowing who this guy was or if he even believed in God. I held my breath and waited for his response.

"Sure," he said, like it was the most natural thing in the world. Joyce and I joined hands and reached out for Kevin's. It was the first real physical contact I'd had with Kevin, and I felt a thrill run through me.

"Bless us, O Lord, and these Thy gifts which we are about to receive from Thy bounty through Christ, Our Lord. Amen"

So, he does know how to pray. It's short and to-the-point and a little on the formal side, but still a prayer.

After dinner, Joyce again pulled out our stash of chocolate chip cookies and we shared them. As darkness fell on the rain forest, small groups of villagers began appearing in the doorway, anxious to talk with Puench. As they spoke, Joyce pulled out a portable cassette tape recorder. With her encouragement, the shy Atshuar women began sending greetings to friends and relatives in other villages. Joyce would broadcast the recorded greetings on her weekly radio show back in Makuma. It didn't take long for the Atshuar women to warm to the task. That left Kevin and me as the only non-Shuar speakers, with no one to talk to but each other.

After an awkward silence, I broke the ice.

"How are you feeling about your time here so far?"

"It's been incredible," he answered, "like something out of a movie. Did you notice how Puancher could move through the jungle without making a sound?"

"Yep, it's amazing," I agreed. "You know, a lot of people who visit here, and even Ecuadorians who live in the cities, think that the Shuar are stupid because they can't speak their language. But they're every bit as intelligent as us. I remember the first time I came down to Ecuador. John came up to Quito to meet me and brought three Shuar men with him."

"Not Joyce?"

"No. She stayed back in Yaapi with the kids. Anyway, it was the first time in their lives the men had left the jungle. It was like they jumped ahead a few centuries, seeing roads, cars and skyscrapers for the first time. It was fun to watch their expressions."

"I'll bet. What a shock."

"Do you know the 'Fav', that supermarket in Quito?"

He looked blank.

"Well, anyway, we went there to buy supplies. Joyce had given John a list, so I offered to help find things. As I turned a corner, I saw all three Shuar men standing in front of a frozen food cooler, giggling like schoolgirls. They kept lowering their hands deep in the freezer, then yanking them out and touching their faces. I laughed, thinking they looked like children. The next day I found out how wrong I was."

"What do you mean?"

"Well, from Quito, we took the road to Shell and spent the night, waiting for an MAF flight back to Yaapi the next morning. After dinner, we went out to the gazebo behind the hospital."

"I know which one you mean. We call it the Auca hut," he said.

"Yeah, well, there was a work team there who were also waiting to get out to the jungle. Most were students at Bible colleges in the U. S. They began asking the Shuar what it was like to live in the rain forest."

"I'll bet that was a real eye-opener for them."

"Yeah, but here's the neat thing. After the students had asked all the questions they could think of one of the Shuar asked if it was okay for him to ask a question, something having to do with God. The Bible students were only too happy to have a chance to enlighten the primitive savages. Know what the question was?"

Kevin shook his head.

"They asked, 'Could you explain to us how there can be three persons in one God?' I've never heard so much throat clearing before in my life. I think the Bible students were amazed that people who looked and sounded so different from them could think just like them."

"How arrogant," he said.

"Maybe, but I find myself thinking the same way. It's easy to think that the Shuar are way behind us since they don't have all our modern conveniences. But being out here makes me realize that if I were on my own, I wouldn't last a week in the jungle."

"You're right. It's amazing anyone can live here. You know, there was a German geologist staying overnight with the Swansons once. He told me that the topsoil supporting the trees in the rain forest averages only eighteen inches in depth. So if you try to clear a field for planting, all the rain just washes the exposed topsoil away. That's why farming doesn't work well here."

After a pause, he went on, "It's weird to think that something like the Amazon rain forest that looks so indestructible is really just a fragile layer covering what's beneath."

"The same could be said for some people."

He ignored my comment and went back to talking about the Shuar.

"Another thing that's been neat is to see their personalities and watch them joke around. They really like to laugh. They seem so much more like real people out here. I must admit that the Shuar I've seen in the hospital remind me more of lab animals than people. They have no personalities that I can see. They just sit stone-faced and even seem a little hostile."

"Can you blame them? Picture living here and getting hurt or sick and then stuck in a flying machine that drops you in a totally unfamiliar place. Pretty soon, people are probing and sticking you with no explanation. I imagine you'd be a little hostile, too."

"Down, girl, I'm on your side. I agree with you."

"Sorry, I didn't mean to bite your head off." I tried to make my voice more pleasant. "It just makes me mad when people think they're so much better than the Indians just because they have a lot more stuff."

"You know, in many ways I wouldn't mind trading places with the Shuar," Kevin said. "Life is so complicated back in the U. S. compared to here. These people have really gotten back to nature."

"Gotten back? They never left."

"I know, but what I mean is, they keep life simple, basic, uncluttered, the way it was meant to be. I just think it's sad when people come in and try to change their way of life."

Suddenly, my suspicions were aroused. "You mean, like Joyce?"

"Hold on now. That's not what I was thinking. Joyce just kind of fits in with the Shuar. I'm talking about people who try to change the way they live."

I wasn't satisfied.

"Look, Joyce gets that all the time from people who visit down here: 'Why can't you just leave these people alone, instead of trying to make them like you?' Well, in the first place, the Shuar live on top of huge oil reserves so, like it or not, their lives are going to change. It's much better that Joyce and people like her who actually care about the Indians help them to get ready for the changes that are coming. Second, how do you know that the Shuar want to stay the same?"

He didn't answer; not that I gave him much of a chance.

"Have you ever considered that maybe they're tired of living in huts and having to hunt for every meal? Who are we to decide what's good for them? Just because we see that modern conveniences come with a price, does that gives us the right to decide it's not for them? You think we get to decide it's better for them to keep living the 'simple life'? Besides, it's not like these people were living in some kind of utopia before the missionaries came. They lived in constant fear and superstition. If it weren't for people like Joyce, they'd still be living that way. Now they live in peace and forgiveness, at least the ones who have become Christians."

Kevin finally spoke up. "I'm glad you mentioned that." He seemed a bit irritated. "That's what I'm talking about. It's fine if you want to help them out, but why do you have to try to change their culture and their beliefs to do it? Besides, do you really think they actually believe all that stuff? Of course, they're going to say they're Christians when missionaries show up here offering them all kinds of goodies."

"You don't have a clue what you're talking about. For your information, Joyce doesn't give anything to the Shuar other than love."

I was fuming. After a brief pause, I went on.

"When we were in Yaapi, I noticed a Shuar man admiring my belt. I took it off to give to him but Joyce stopped me. She said he would lose dignity if I just gave it to him, so instead I traded it for some feather earrings he made."

There was silence. I thought of something else he needed to know.

"Besides, it's not just about changing the way they live, it's about where they spend eternity."

That got him riled. "That's another thing I have trouble with. If what you say is true, what about all the Indians who never heard of Jesus? Did they all get sent to hell? What kind of loving God is that?"

I couldn't believe what I was hearing.

"So you think God has to explain Himself to you? For your information, I don't know what happens to those people. I don't have to answer to God for other people's decisions, but He will hold me accountable for how I respond to Him. And, by the way, the same is true for you."

I guess the tone of voice we were using alerted Joyce to an impending crisis, because just then she poked her head around the corner of the room divider and asked cheerily, "Anybody ready for another cookie?"

Joyce skillfully re-directed the conversation, and soon we were all laughing about our fishing disaster. Just before we turned in for the night, Kevin said to Joyce:

"I've seen lots of women, children and young men, but no older men. Where are they?"

"Its funny," Joyce replied, "I was thinking of that yesterday when you said what a pleasant, peaceful life the people have here. It hasn't always been that way. When John and I first arrived here and began working with the Shuar, there still were occasional revenge killings like in the old days. It's hard to imagine now, but a generation ago these people lived in constant fear. Their lives were controlled by a dark spirit world. It was a terrible way to live."

"But they don't live that way anymore. Why not? What changed?"

"Well, for one thing the government of Ecuador outlawed the practice of shrinking heads. That had been a part of the ritual of taking revenge on your enemy I haven't seen a shrunken head for more than ten years."

"Oh, I see," Kevin said, nodding his head.

Joyce went on, "But I'd like to think that, more importantly, the Shuar have been introduced to the love and forgiveness of Christ."

Kevin didn't respond. I wondered what he was thinking. Did he acknowledge the life-changing power of the gospel? Or was he one of those people who believed that man was basically good and, if given the chance, would choose to live a life of peace? His face gave no hint of what was going on in his mind.

After a long pause, he said softly, "This has been a fun couple of days, Joyce. Thanks for letting me tag along with you."

"Well, we've enjoyed having you, haven't we, Leslie?"

I mumbled something in reply and threw myself on my sleeping bag.

Leslie, you dope. Why do you always have to argue with people? Why can't you be more loving toward others, like Joyce?

I went back and forth in my mind, trying to convince myself that, really, what I had done was okay, because it was God I was defending rather than myself. It even seemed that Joyce had defended me but, deep down, I knew that what really set me off was the realization that this guy, about whom I had been building all sorts of hopes, was not going to be God's answer for my future after all. I wasn't even sure if he believed in God. My dreams had hit a snag.

Looks like I'm back to square one. Now what? Where do I go from here?

Chapter 17
Kevin's Chance

It rained hard that night, and the next day dawned with a chill in the air. It was Sunday, but the morning Bible teaching session was not remarkably different than the previous ones. The only noticeable innovation was that, near the end of the service, about twenty Atshuar came to the front of the lodge where Joyce had just made some sort of invitation. She beamed as she addressed those who remained seated, from time to time gesturing toward the group up front who stood staring at the dirt floor.

Leslie, who until that moment had been pretty much ignoring me, leaned over to say, "All those people want to be saved." I could tell from her voice that she was thrilled at the prospect, so I refrained from asking, "Saved from what?"

I still had a leftover bad feeling from the night before. I knew I had said something I shouldn't have, but I wasn't sure what it was.

By the time we had finished lunch, the temperature had warmed considerably and I was ready for a nap.

Just as I was beginning to doze, Joyce announced, "I'm going for a swim. Do you two want to join me?"

At that point I wasn't really all that interested, but I thought,

Hey, this might be a chance to see Leslie in something more revealing than those baggy dresses and funky tights she wears.

I waited to let Leslie make the first move and when she agreed to go, I announced, "I'm game. Just give me a minute to put my suit on."

When I reappeared, both women were standing outside waiting for me, still dressed in their baggy, calf-length outfits and rubber galoshes.

"Where are your bathing suits?" I asked.

"You're looking at them," Joyce answered, laughing. "When in Shuar land, do as the Shuar do."

I was stuck. Obviously, at that point I couldn't very well say, "Well, frankly, I'm not that interested in swimming, it's just that I was hoping to see more of Leslie's body," so I had no alternative but to trudge off toward the river with my fully– clothed companions.

At Joyce's suggestion, rather than enter the river at the nearest point, we followed a parallel trail several hundred yards upriver.

"That way we can just float downstream and get out of the river close to home," she observed.

We waded in and distanced ourselves from the shore. I was surprised by how strong the current felt. In no time we were swept off our feet, being carried downriver. We soon overtook a large log off to one side, also being taken by the current.

"Come on, let's ride it," Joyce yelled above the din of the river.

We reached it and took turns trying to mount the log which twirled around with each new change in weight distribution. Just about the time we succeeded in draping all three of our bodies atop the log, we looked up to see trouble headed our way. We were fast approaching a sharp bend where the river changed course to run parallel with the airstrip. It was obvious that our waterlogged craft was not going to make the turn. Instead it was on a collision course with dead trees and other debris trapped in the eddy currents at the river's bend.

"Abandon ship! Abandon ship!" I called with mock alarm.

Leslie and I pushed away from the floating log and caught on to a branch protruding from the water just before the turn.

"Joyce! What are you doing?" yelled Leslie. "Get off there before it crashes."

"I can't. I'm stuck," Joyce called back, laughing.

We watched for a moment to see if she would free herself. When she did not, Leslie said with some urgency, "You'd better go help her."

I launched myself back into the current in the direction of Joyce's log. Leslie, meanwhile, also let loose of the branch we had been clutching and was propelled downriver. Joyce's raft rammed a stationary log lying perpendicular to the one she was riding. This caused her log to swing in an arc and soon she was heading downriver again, backwards. By the time I joined her on the log she was animated and laughing.

"Wow, what a ride!"

We continued downriver a little ways. Following instinct born of years spent swimming in Ecuador's treacherous rivers, Joyce looked around to see where Leslie was. Her smiling face turned to a look of concern as she searched in vain for a glimpse of Leslie. Suddenly, the concern on her face turned to panic. Pointing back upstream she screamed,

"Leslie!"

Chapter 18
Leslie's Drowning

Something deep in the water grabbed me.

I was floating upright with legs beneath the water, facing downriver, ahead of Joyce and Kevin. I laughed hard as I looked over my shoulder to watch their antics with the log. Suddenly, my legs and lower torso were held tight. The strong current pushed my head forward beneath the surface. I flailed my arms and fought to bring my head up to gulp air.

At first, I wasn't worried and even laughed at my predicament. Here I was, trying to be so modest wearing this ridiculous pants-dress, and now it was caught on something in the river. I figured I would just pull it free and be on my way. I ducked under the surface, reached down and tugged. There was no give. I opened my eyes underwater to figure out what the problem was, but it was no use – the brown, churning water admitted no light. As I began to re-surface for more air, I felt a clunk on the back of my shoulders, forcing me down into the water. Confused at first, I soon realized what had happened. The log that Joyce and Kevin were on was passing over me. It soon was gone, freeing me to return to my efforts to reach the surface. Desperate to refresh the oxygen-depleted air in my lungs, I arched my back, pulling my face into sunlight with all the strength I had in my arms.

As I broke the surface, I realized that I should have exhaled on the way up. Instead, I had to waste precious time expelling air from my lungs before sucking in what little air I could in the time remaining before gravity and the current pulled me back under. In a split second I had to decide whether to expend the effort to re-surface for more air, or use what little I had to free myself from whatever held me. Curling myself upside down against the current, I once again grabbed the hem of my dress and pulled with all my might. There was no give.

As my wearying arms fought to bring my face back to the life-giving air above the pitiless swirl, fear began to invade the outer reaches of my consciousness. All sense of humor and irony at my predicament faded. It was replaced instead by memories of the summer worker who had drowned in Puyupungo. It was not the depth of the water that killed him – by all accounts, it was only up to his knees – but rather the strength of the treacherous current., dragging him under.

Stay calm. Don't panic.

This time I remembered to exhale on the way up. I was rewarded with a full expansion of my lungs as my mouth broke the surface and opened wide to gasp in the sweet, sweet air.

With renewed strength, I dived down, fighting against the relentless current, trying once again to reach whatever it was that was holding me. I couldn't get to it. My straining muscles were no match for the tireless force of falling water. I tried again, and again. Each effort only sapped my remaining strength. My lungs ached. I realized there was very little time left before I would be forced to expel the air trapped in my lungs. Once that happened, my reflexes would cause me to inhale, sucking brown water rather than clear air into my lungs. The life-giving flow of oxygen to my brain would be shut off. I would die. Somehow, this realization, rather than inciting panic, removed it. A deep sense of peace came over me. Time seemed to slow down.

Almost reluctantly, I roused myself from my half-dream. I remembered where I was and what was happening. I realized that I had to do something. Gathering all the strength that remained in my weary body, I lunged back. At last I felt the cause of my desperate situation. The jagged branch of a submerged log had trapped the leg of my pants-dress. I tore at it, trying to free myself from this death trap. But the more I pulled, the deeper the branch plunged through the hole in my pants. All my efforts were in vain. My situation was hopeless. I surrendered to the force of the current, allowing it to stretch me out face down, just beneath the water's surface.

Just then, I felt strong hands grab me. Someone had hold of my hair, pulling it and forcing my head backwards and up, up until my face broke the barrier between my watery grave and the living earth. The warmth of the sunlight was like a magnet, pulling my face up and reviving me. With mouth wide opened, I sucked in air. I became conscious of movement around me. The strong arms were now around my lower waist. Without warning, my head was jerked once again beneath the surface. Something was pulling me against the cruel current that was trying so hard to suck the breath from me. I was faintly conscious of a titanic battle going on around me – a life and death struggle – with me as the prize. How long the contest continued, I have no clear recollection. All I remember is that all of a sudden I was upright, hurtling downstream. Spasms of coughing alternated with great gulps of air. Someone was with me, behind me, holding me above the water. I turned my head to see who my rescuer was. There he was! Kevin wasn't looking at me. With a grim look of determination, he was scanning the river bank for a place to come ashore. One arm clutched me around my waist, holding my limp body close to his. With the other, he began side-stroking toward the bank. I felt the power in his hold and relaxed as he carried me along. He guided me out of the current without effort, or so it seemed.

"I'm okay, I'm okay," I sputtered as we reached shallow water.

We both collapsed on the muddy bank, panting for breath.

"Are you sure you're okay?" The look of concern on his face made me want to cry.

"Yes, really, I'm fine – now."

I lay back against the bank in order to take bigger breaths. Soon, I was able to speak in sentences.

"Kevin, thank you. That was such a close call. I don't know how much longer I could have held on until you got to me. You saved my life!"

"Well, let's not get over-dramatic about it."

"No, I mean I was in real trouble before you got there. When I first got caught I was laughing so hard I couldn't take a full breath. It took me a while to realize how much danger I was in."

"Happy to be of service," he smiled. Then, after a pause, "It's funny. I spent the first couple of summers in high school as a life guard and never had to save anyone. Then, I no sooner meet you, and you go out and try to drown yourself. You gave Joyce quite a scare."

I didn't ask if it gave him a scare, too. I doubted he would have admitted it if it had. But, I didn't need to know his thoughts. It was enough that he had acted.

He stood and offered his hand to help me up. There was a low bluff with an oblique footpath leading from where we stood at water's edge to higher ground. With one hand he supported my elbow, and the other he placed with the base of his palm in the small of my back, as his fingers wrapped around my waist. My soaked dress that had seemed so formidable an obstacle moments earlier melted away at his touch. My body shuddered, my knees nearly buckled. I leaned against him, grateful for his support. I felt so safe and warm, nestled against him. All too soon we reached the top of the bluff where Joyce had just arrived from having exited the river farther downstream. Kevin released me into Joyce's enthusiastic bear hug.

"Leslie, praise God you're safe! How do you feel? Are you all right?"

"Yes, Joyce, I'm fine. Don't worry."

As soon as she could see that I was unharmed, she pulled me to one side and whispered in my ear, "Leslie, he swam upriver to get to you – I mean, against the current. I've never seen anything like it!"

"Well, I'm glad he was there," was all I could think to say, trying hard to suppress the thrill I was feeling. I didn't need Joyce to convince me what a hero he was. The question I pondered was whether or not he would have accomplished the same feat for anyone, or did he have an extra measure of strength because it was me?

The three of us walked back single file on the narrow, muddy trail through the forest toward the airstrip, with Joyce leading.

"Wait a second," I said as I placed a hand on Kevin's shoulder in front of me. I bent my knee, almost touching my heel to my buttock, and emptied a gush of river water from my upside down boot. Kevin turned around in time to see me repeating the procedure with my other boot.

"Well, I'm relieved," he smiled. "You'll never guess what I thought you were doing back there."

I laughed. "Hey, listen to this," I said as I began to suck my belly in and push it out in rapid succession. It sounded like a half-full gasoline can sloshing around.

"Oh, that's very attractive," he joked. His smile was accompanied by a twinkle in his eye.

That evening Kevin and I sat on the floor of the hut as Joyce recorded greetings that would be played on the Macuma radio station. At one point, as I was writing in my journal, Kevin reached out and gently pinched my toe to get my attention. He smiled and winked at me when I looked up. A warm feeling surged through me. I couldn't help but feel that something had happened that day that would forever change things between us. That night I drifted off to sleep with the memory of his arm around me and that captivating wink.

Chapter 19
Kevin's Discovery

There was no denying it. I was becoming more and more captivated by this forthright and unpretentious young woman. However, time was not on my side. Soon we would part ways to return to our own separate lives. The chances of our ever seeing one another again were negligible. Despite that fact, I found myself that evening memorizing her parents' address as she carefully wrote it on an envelope containing film she was sending home to be developed.

Monday dawned bright and clear. It was hard to believe our time in Kapawari was coming to an end. It had all gone so fast. That morning, in a break from the routine, the villagers met at the river rather than at the tribal lodge. The reason soon became apparent. We assembled at a point in the river beyond the far end of the airstrip, where another sharp bend created a slow-flowing shallow pool. After an opening prayer and the singing of a number of hymns, a score of Atshuar followed Ernesto into the still water. I recognized them as the same group that had gone to the front of the lodge the day before. They took turns addressing a few words to the people left standing on the bank and were then submerged in the pool by Ernesto. I had never seen anything like it. The only baptisms I witnessed were done in a church, by a priest, on a little baby. In some ways this made a lot more sense having a willing participant. I liked the natural setting better, too. But for just some guy, rather than a priest, to perform the ceremony – somehow it just didn't seem right.

Baptism in the Kapawari River

At the conclusion of the service each of the Atshuar came to say goodbye to Puench, Maswink and me. It was a touching scene as each came, shook our hands and rattled on in Shuar as if we all understood them. The words were undecipherable to me, but the feelings were clear. One-by-one or in small groups they trudged back to their dwellings beneath the canopy of the rain forest. This brief interlude in the routine of their lives was now over. Soon we were left standing alone.

"Well, guess we better go pack," said Joyce. "We want to be ready for Dave when he comes."

"I wish we could just stay here," I sighed.

"It has been a lot of fun, hasn't it?" said Leslie.

There wasn't much to pack, although Leslie and I had each purchased a blowgun as a souvenir of our time. The Atshuar could only spare one quiver to sell and it was not in the best of condition. Leslie bought it anyway, knowing that the Shuar who lived in Makuma could repair it for her. She had earlier purchased another quiver which was still at Joyce's house, so she proposed to run in and get it for me when we landed in Makuma to drop off her and Joyce.

It took me a little while to organize and pack up what was left of the medical supplies I had brought. When I came outside, neither of the women was anywhere in sight. I sat on a stump for a short time, thinking they would show up at any minute. When they did not, I decided to go in search of them. I crossed the airstrip and headed for the river. As I came to the water's edge, there was Leslie. She was sitting on the trunk of a tree which was leaning out over the bend in the river that had almost proved our undoing the day before.

"Hi. Where's Joyce?" I asked, surprised at not seeing them together.

"Oh, she wanted to stay and listen for any message that might come over the radio. If the weather is bad in Shell they'll try to let us know, so we're not waiting all day for them to come.," she answered.

I took up a position on a rock a respectable distance away. We both stared at the river.

Finally, she broke the silence. "You told Joyce you wished you could stay here. Did you mean that? Do you think you could ever see yourself living in a place like this? I mean, really."

I began to tell her about the books I'd read by Tom Dooley and how that was the inspiration for me wanting to become a doctor. I figured she'd be impressed by that.

"But," I admitted, "I'd kind of forgotten about all that until I came down here."

"Oh? Why was that?"

"I don't know – a bunch of things."

"Like what?" she persisted. It was obvious that she was not going to let me off the hook until I came up with a better reason.

"Well, for one thing, after college I was engaged to a girl who didn't seem all that thrilled when I bounced the idea off her," I offered, hoping that would end the Inquisition. Fat chance.

"You *were* engaged? You mean you're not anymore?"

"No," I answered, "we broke it off about a year ago."

"Do you mean she broke it off, or you did?" My discomfort was growing.

"I did."

Leslie paused to consider. I saw my chance and took it. "What about you?" I asked, turning the tables. "Any serious boyfriends?"

"I've had lots of boyfriends, but not anything I would call real serious."

Hmm, there are possibilities here.

"What about now, though?" I bore in, hoping to keep the initiative.

Now she seemed to be squirming a bit. "I'm dating a guy back in California." She paused and then continued matter-of-factly, "I think he wants to marry me."

I was stunned. With one sentence she had torn up by the roots the tender shoot of my mind's fantasy.

Trying to show no emotion, I observed, "Oh, I see. Well, I'm glad it's nothing real serious, anyway."

She didn't respond. Just then, I heard the familiar drone of a Cessna engine.

"I guess we better get back to the airstrip," I said, grateful for the distraction.

I looked up and saw her staring at the river, but not focusing on it. Her mind was far, far away. Her face was dappled by the sun filtering through the forest canopy. I was struck by her serene beauty.

"Leslie," I whispered, "did you hear me? Its time to go."

Chapter 20
Leslie's Departure

Let's see, where are we here?

I was trying to sift through all the new information I had just received and make sense of it. My mind was whirring.

Number one, he's single. That's good. Number two, he apparently doesn't have a girlfriend right now.

I realized I didn't know that for sure, but it seemed that way.

He's really interested in missions. He's not just saying that. That's the reason he wanted to study medicine in the first place.

My mind began reconstructing a future built around him.

Slow down, Leslie. You don't even know if he's interested in you.

Then again, that was a big part of the reason I went down to the river by myself. I figured if he was at all interested in me, he'd find me. And he did! I went back to dreaming.

Could he be God's answer to my prayers?

I was a little ashamed of myself for being so surprised. After all, aren't we supposed to pray believing that God …

Wait a minute. Hold everything. Come to think of it, I don't even know for sure if he believes in God. Well, I'll just have to ask him.

From somewhere far away I heard his voice.

"What?" I said aloud. "What did you say?"

His gentle voice bridged the narrow gap between us.

"I said its time to go. There's the plane."

"Oh, of course. I'm coming."

He reached out his hand for mine and helped me off the log. We hurried single-file toward the airstrip. As we neared the clearing he waited to give me a chance to exit the jungle alone. By now he knew of the Shuar cultural taboos against two single people of the opposite sex being alone in the jungle together. It was just one more thoughtful act that attracted me to him.

"Maybe I'll get a chance to talk to him about his relationship with God during our flight," I schemed.

Joyce arrived at the hut just as I did. In a minute, the Cessna was on the ground, rolling to a stop right in front of us. All three of us ran out to the plane with our gear. Dave lowered himself from the cockpit.

"Change of plans," he shouted. "I've got too much weight to take all of you at once. I'll take the ladies to Makuma, then come back to pick you up, Kevin. Let's get going. Times-a- wasting."

Dave rushed to help me get strapped in the rear seat. There was a Shuar woman in the seat next to me. We smiled at one another. Joyce sat in the co-pilot's seat. Kevin stepped up to the still-opened door.

"Joyce, thank you so much. This has been a weekend I will never forget."

He turned to say something to me, but just then there was a commotion outside. The crowd of onlookers parted and a young Atshuar man came up holding in both hands a turtle the size of a frying pan. He elbowed past Kevin, jabbering to Joyce who relayed the message to Dave. Dave rolled his eyes, and then nodded agreement. The Atshuar man reached across me to place the turtle on the floor of the plane behind my seat. The door was shut and we started moving.

It was all happening so fast. I realized I might never see him again. Tears began welling up. I wanted to get another look at Kevin, but I was afraid he would see the tears in my eyes. Joyce didn't help matters.

"Wow, what a great weekend! Wasn't Dr. Tivi just wonderful? Did you see how he was with the people, so kind and gentle? And what a nice sense of humor. Then, to top it off, the way he rescued you from drowning! Oh, my."

Why couldn't she just be quiet? I was glad that she wasn't able to see me seated behind her, tears streaming down my cheeks. Just to be certain, I turned around pretending to be interested in the turtle. I chided myself for the ridiculous emotional reaction I was having. It made no sense. I hardly knew the guy, yet I felt as if my heart was breaking. I couldn't explain the total sense of loss I felt at leaving Kevin behind. By the time we were barreling down the runway for take-off, I stole one last glance at Kapawari. There he was! Head and shoulders above the crowd, waving and smiling. Then, just like that, he disappeared from view.

Will I ever see him again?

Chapter 21
Kevin's Quiver

Back in Shell, I threw myself into my work. I had less than four weeks remaining in my time here and I wanted to make the most of it. It was not difficult to stay busy. The pace at the hospital had become more intense. There were a number of contributing factors. One, of course, was the specter of Wally's imminent departure and all the adjustments that would entail. Another was related to the normal ebb and flow of patients. It seemed that there were always either too many patients or too few, never a comfortable steady flow. At this time we were on the up side of the cycle.

Also, there was a sense of anticipation in the air. A team of working visitors was due to arrive soon. From what I could gather, there was an Ecuadorian physician, Dr. Luis Vasconez, who was a renowned Professor of Plastic & Reconstructive Surgery at Emory University in Atlanta. Some part of his early medical training had taken place at HCJB's hospital in Quito. Dr. Vasconez maintained a relationship with HCJB and almost every summer brought a group of fellow surgeons and residents-in-training with him back to Ecuador in order to donate their skills to Ecuador's poor. Much effort was required in anticipation of their arrival. Word would need to be spread throughout the region of the availability of their services and date of arrival. Patients had to be seen and evaluated for suitability for surgery. Clinic spaces and schedules would be modified to accommodate the additional workers. Arrangements needed to be made for transportation, food and lodging.

Although I was aware of the heightened tension caused by these impending changes, none of it was my responsibility, and so my daily routine changed little. I went back to dividing my time between outpatient clinics, ward duties and assisting in the operating room. As so often happened, the routine was interrupted one morning by an emergency. John and I received word in the operating room that Wally had just gotten a call from Carol Osterhus. Dave was on his way back from the jungle with a badly injured patient. No other details were available.

Later, just as we were finishing the operation, Lois Price poked her head in the OR and said, "Wally asked me to let you know, the patient from the jungle is here in the emergency room. He'll need to go to the OR. He blew his hand off with dynamite."

As always, Lois' demeanor was calm regardless of the intensity of the circumstances.

"Why don't you break scrub to go help Wally," John said, "while I finish up here?"

When I arrived in the ER I wasn't prepared for what I saw. There on the gurney laid a Shuar man of about my age. His face, neck and chest were freckled with what appeared to be embedded bits of gunpowder. What remained of his left hand was dangling over a basin. Wally was gently washing the mangled mess with a yellow antibiotic solution. The patient's thumb, index finger and most of his long finger were missing. Blood, mixed with the antibiotic rinse, was pouring from the wound into the basin. The man lay still, not making a sound, his face impassive.

For the first time since my arrival in Shell I saw this Shuar man as a fellow human being rather than a clinical specimen. He looked very much like several of the young men in Kapawari who showed Maswink and me how to use a blowgun and who laughed aloud at my inept attempt. How would this man hunt now? He probably had a wife and children. Could he continue to provide for them?

"*Pujamek*," I greeted him. He nodded in response.

"What happened?" I asked Wally.

"He was fishing with dynamite and it went off in his hand," was his reply.

"But I thought the Shuar used poison?"

"Yes, traditionally they do. But as others have moved into the rain forest, the Shuar have learned that dynamite can accomplish the same purpose without their having to search the forest for *barbasco*." He sounded disgusted. "We see these injuries not infrequently. The problem is that the fuse gets wet in the river. When they go to light it, it doesn't look like anything is happening. But the powder inside the fuse is burning. As they're getting ready to light another match, the dynamite explodes and this is what you get."

The man was wheeled to the operating room. Irene prayed with him in Spanish before administering the anesthetic. I helped John clean the wound as best we could, removing dead tissue and other debris from it. We wrapped it in a bulky sterile dressing. John tied a kind of cloth sleeve around the patient's forearm. The sleeve had long ties coming off the end of it that could be fastened to an IV pole, in order to elevate the injured hand. My mind was churning the whole time we were working in silence.

When we finished the case, I went to find Wally in the clinic. He was alone in one of the offices, reading a medical text.

"Could I interrupt you for a second?" I asked.

"Sure. Come on in, have a seat." He indicated a chair. "What's up?"

"Well…" I hesitated, and then plunged into it. "I've been doing a lot of thinking," I began. "To be honest, when I first came here, I wasn't crazy about the idea that this was a mission hospital I would be working at. It's kind of embarrassing to say that now."

I hesitated. Wally gave me an encouraging smile.

"Anyway, like I say, I've been doing some thinking and I was wondering. If you had it to do over again, what do you think would be the best kind of training to have to come and work in a place like this?"

Wally thought for a moment.

"Well," he said, "I think I would do one of two things. I'd either come down right after internship, since a lot of what you do here is different than what you do in the U. S., and you can learn what you need to know after you get here. Or else, if I was going to do some sort of further training, I would do a general surgery residency. I think that would be the best preparation for what I'd be likely to encounter here."

I pondered his reply. "Okay, thanks," I said, standing up, "that's all I wanted to know. I'll let you get back to your studying. Thanks again."

"You're welcome. Anything else?" he asked with a tone of expectancy.

"Nope, that's it."

I was glad to escape the room when I did. I realized that I had made myself vulnerable. I felt certain that, had Charlotte been present, she would have encouraged Wally to go for the kill. For now, I was happy to circle the snare.

The truth was that there was a lot more on my mind, but I just didn't feel like talking about it. I realized that, as skeptical as I had been, little by little I was being won over by these people I had been rubbing shoulders with the past couple of months. It wasn't the result of any great theological arguments. There was just something about the way they lived their lives. Two months earlier, if anyone had asked me if I felt like something was missing in my life, I would have scoffed at the idea. After all, I was young. I was healthy. I had a brilliant and lucrative career in front of me. So it came as a surprise when I realized that these people had something in their lives that was missing in mine. As the days passed, I came to recognize what it was. They each possessed a sense of purpose for their lives that went beyond themselves. I wanted that for myself. I just wasn't at all sure I was ready to buy into the whole "accept Jesus as Lord and Savior" routine.

Soon after my conversation with Wally, we received word that, due to unforeseen circumstances, Dr. Vasconez was not going to be able to make the trip to Shell. He was sending one of his residents in his place. Dr. Lou Hill was in his next-to-last year of general surgery residency. He arrived in Shell without fanfare and right away set about scheduling patients for surgery. He had a particular interest in cleft lip repairs in children. Lou had recently completed a plastic surgery rotation with Dr. Vasconez, during which time he had learned to perform that delicate and complicated procedure.

I didn't like dealing with babies with cleft lips. To me, it was such an obvious and hideous deformity that I wanted to divert my gaze. The condition is caused by a failure of the upper lip to fuse properly during development *in utero*. The baby is born with a gaping defect to one or both sides of the midline. The gap runs right up into the nose, which is usually flattened on that side. Through the defect can be seen the mucous-covered gums and, in the case of older children, misshapen teeth. It's a horrible deformity that, if left untreated, sentences the child to a lifetime of curious stares and social ostracism.

I was assigned to assist Lou while John operated on other patients in the second operating room. I was fascinated by the meticulous little flaps of skin and muscle that Lou created to bridge the gap in the patient's lip. The transformation that occurred in the patient's appearance after a couple of hours of operating was astounding. And that was with the sutures still in place. Several days later, when the sutures were removed, I couldn't believe it was the same patient. The incisions had been carefully placed so as to make them as inconspicuous as possible. Lou's knowledge and skill changed that baby's future.

Lou and I talked while we worked. I told him of my experiences in Kapawari. He became very interested in getting out to the jungle. There were no flights available on such short notice, so instead I offered to take him to a mission outpost called Puyupungu, which could be reached by road. Lois Price had taken me there on a previous weekend.

On Saturday, Lou and I boarded a bus in Shell for the hour's ride to the place where the road ended at a washed-out bridge over the Pastaza River. At that spot was located a *taravita*, a home made cable car that transported pedestrians across the river. A thick steel cable was suspended from concrete towers on either side of the swirling river far below. Attached to the cable by overhead pulleys was a simple wooden platform. A group of four or five passengers would stand on the platform and hang on to whatever they could grasp. All too frequently, what they grasped by reflex was the cable just in front of the moving pulley. Earlier in my time at the hospital we had received patients with terrible hand injuries that they said were caused by the *taravita*. Now I understood why. The men working the *taravita* would sling it as far as it would go along the cable. As it slowed to a stop near the low point of the cable's arc, workers on the far side of the river would begin hauling on a long rope attached to the suspended platform. It made for a thrilling ride.

Once we reached safety on the other side, we began an hour's hike along a muddy jungle trail until we reached another unspanned river. Here we shouted to a man on the opposite side. After a while, he brought his dugout canoe across. After negotiating and paying the five sucre fare, we loaded in the canoe and were soon deposited on the other side of the swift-flowing river. Another forty-five minutes of slogging through calf-deep mud brought us to the little jungle community of Puyupungu.

I had been interested to learn from Lois that one of the five martyred missionaries had once lived here. Newly-weds Jim and Betty Elliott made their first home in Puyupungu. On my previous visit we had encountered many smiling Shuar, all anxious to converse in Spanish with Lois. This time, however, as Lou and I approached, there was an eerie silence. The village was completely deserted. We shouted out greetings but received no reply. The place looked like a ghost town. Throughout our visit to Puyupungu we never saw another soul there and never learned the reason why.

The village was located on a high bluff overlooking the convergence of two rivers. One was the swift-moving river we had crossed by canoe, the other a smaller, lazier stream. In exploring the latter, we found an abandoned dugout canoe and launched it. We had real difficulty keeping our balance as we stood to pole it across the water. The setting was surreal – bright, blue sky, dense tropical vegetation spilling out over the serpentine waterway, the stillness broken only by the hum of jungle insects.

"Wow, what a setting!" Lou exclaimed. "Here, take my camera and get a picture of me poling this canoe in the Amazon jungle."

I did as instructed and pointed the lens in his direction, ready to shoot.

"Wait, not yet," he said. With that, he dropped his pants, underwear and all, to his ankles where they couldn't be seen from the camera angle. "Now," he said as he stood buck naked in the bow of the dugout with his back toward me, straining against the pole.

"Perfect," I laughed. "This will make it into National Geographic – 'rare albino Amazon Indian in his natural habitat.'"

That was Lou, always looking for the fun in life. One afternoon back in Shell when we had finished in the OR for the day, he proposed we take a stroll through town.

As we passed a dingy bar he suggested, "Let's get a beer."

I went in with him and sat down but soon began suffering pangs of conscience. After all, I had signed that pledge in Dave Reifsnyder's office – it seemed like years ago and a million miles away. I remembered at the time thinking that it was such a juvenile, hypocritical requirement. Who cares if I have a beer if I want one? On the other hand, the people in Shell had been so nice to me; I wouldn't want to disappoint them. It was different for Lou. He hadn't been here long enough for the townspeople to know who he was. I was torn. At last, I decided.

"It's my life and if I want a beer I can have one. It's nobody's business but mine."

Just then the waiter came up. "*Dos cervezas*," I said, holding up two fingers.

"So, what do you think about these missionaries?" Lou wanted to know.

"Well, they're definitely unusual."

"That's for sure," Lou interrupted. "But you kind of have to admire them."

"Yeah, I've talked to them a lot during my time here. There are differences between them, but there are a few things they all seem to agree on."

"Like what?"

"First, they all know for sure there's a God. And not just any God, it's got to be the one talked about in the Bible. Second, they're all convinced that God sent Jesus Christ to die in order to make a way for all of us worthless sinners to get into heaven. And last, even though they're sure they've got a free ticket to heaven, they think it really matters to God how they live their lives. One of them, I think it was John, told me, 'It's got to be more than just saying you're a Christian. Just because you belong to the Lions' Club, doesn't make you a lion'. I thought that was pretty good."

After a while, Lou and I got around to talking about future plans as we sat drinking. I told him of my intention to do a pediatric residency.

"Really?" he asked. "I kinda figured you for the surgeon type. You seem pretty comfortable in the OR."

With that, I confessed that I was having second thoughts but figured it was too late now to find a decent surgery program to get into.

"Why don't you apply to Grady Hospital, where I am," Lou suggested. "It couldn't hurt. If you're not accepted, then you can do peds somewhere."

"Well, maybe I will."

"You can stay in my apartment when you come up for an interview."

"**If** I get invited for an interview."

The following Monday morning, as I was entering the hospital for rounds, Lois Price was seated at the nurses' station.

"You've got mail, Doctor Tivi," she teased. I was taken aback. I hadn't told anyone in Shell about my Shuar name.

Showing as little emotion as possible, I went to look in my assigned mailbox. I had grown unaccustomed to checking. The only mail I had received in the ten weeks I had been here were a couple of letters from my mother and a notice that I had passed, by the skin of my teeth, the basic science portion of the National Boards test I had taken months before. Mail to or from the U. S. required about six weeks' transit time.

In my mailbox I found a yellow plastic bag with a note attached to the outside, addressed to "Doctor Tivi (Kevin Kerrigan)". Inside the bag I found a blowgun quiver, complete with curare-tipped darts. I felt my pulse quicken as I tore open the envelope. Inside was a handwritten note on lined notebook paper. It read:

> *Dear Doctor Tivi,*
>
> *Here is the quiver I promised you. I'm sending it on the next flight out. I hope it makes it to you before you leave.*
>
> *Joyce and I are getting ready to go up to Quito for the GMU conference that starts on the 16th of this month.*
>
> *Hope your last weeks in Shell are good. It was fun having you along on our trip. I enjoyed talking with you.*
>
> *Leslie*

A flood of memories of our time together in Kapawari washed over me.

Chapter 22
Leslie's Jolt

"Maswink! Venga a la clinica, rápido!"

Tzamaren, one of the Shuar who worked in the broadcasting studio with Joyce, was clearly agitated. But if he thought speaking Spanish rather than Shuar would make me understand him any better, he was mistaken. There was no mistaking his tone of voice and animated gestures, however. I ran behind him past the Drown house, in the direction of the clinic. I began to see clues as to why Tzamaren was so excited. Large drops of blood led up the steps. It took a moment for my eyes to adjust as I entered the dark room, but there was no missing the blood-soaked shirt bundled up on the floor. On the exam table lay a Shuar man, with Joyce hovering over him. It was hard to say who looked more ashen.

"Leslie, thank God you're here!" My pulse, already racing, quickened.

Joyce was clutching the man's left forearm, pressing hard on a wad of gauze. A slight grimace stole across his stoic face.

"What happened?" I demanded, fighting to remain calm.

"Machete wound." Joyce was struggling to hold the gauze in place without having to look at the injured arm.

"Can he still move all his fingers?"

"I don't know. I think so. Let me ask."

Through Joyce's translation and my gestures, we were able to assure ourselves that the patient could bend and straighten his thumb and each of his fingers.

"Good," I said, trying to sound confident. "It doesn't look like he's damaged any of his tendons. Now let's check his pulses." They, too, were intact.

"This doesn't look so bad. Let's take a look at the wound itself."

Joyce lifted the gauze to expose a 2-inch gash running diagonally across the back of the man's forearm. The wound gaped open to expose what looked like chicken fat on either side with clotted blood in the depths. There was very little active bleeding.

"Looks like you stopped the bleeding with the pressure you applied," I reassured Joyce. "Of course, you almost fractured his forearm in the process with your death grip."

The tension melted from Joyce's face as we laughed. She even stole a glance at the wound.

"Can you sew it up?"

"Me?" I asked, trying not to appear too shocked.

"Yes, you. Who else?"

"Joyce, I've never done suturing before. I've only seen it being done. I'm not even sure how to do it."

"Well, he wants you to sew it up."

"How long ago did he cut it?"

"He says it happened this morning. It took him a couple of hours to come upriver."

Joyce could tell I was still hesitant. "I doubt we could get a plane in here this afternoon and, even if we could, it would cost him a lot of money to go to Shell."

"Well, maybe," I wavered. "What do you have in the way of instruments and suture?"

"That's great! I knew you could do it," Joyce proclaimed. She turned to the patient and rattled off something in Shuar, which caused the man's face to break out in a grin. I was stuck.

Joyce helped me find everything I needed but then turned to go.

"Aren't you going to at least stay and help me? After all, you're the one who got me into this."

"I would really like to, Leslie, but I can't – doctor's orders."

I thought she was just being smart and felt a bit offended until we spoke about it later that evening.

"Leslie, thank you so much for what you did today. The man was very grateful, and so am I. I don't know what I would have done if you hadn't been here."

"I'm sure you could have done just as good yourself."

"Well."

"What?"

"Well," she repeated. "You could have done just as well. It's an adverb, not an adjective."

Joyce was always correcting my grammar. I didn't mind, even though I still didn't understand the difference.

"No, Leslie," she continued, "I couldn't have. Not now. Maybe a few years ago, but not now."

"What do you mean, Joyce? You're a nurse, too."

I knew that John and Joyce had attended Biola's School of Missionary Medicine prior to coming down to Ecuador. Completion of the program resulted in certification as a licensed vocational nurse.

Joyce explained. "When we first came to Yaapi, right away we had Shuar coming from all over the place looking for medical help. I was so glad we had taken the course at Biola before we came, because there is no way to avoid being the medical expert here. You know how it is. If you have a white face, they assume you know something about medicine. John was very good at it and enjoyed it. I liked it, too, as long as I could help him. But when I came back after John's death, one of the jobs I was given here in Makuma was to be in charge of the clinic. I used to dread hearing that there was a patient waiting for me who was beyond the care that the health promoter could give. Pretty soon after I got here I began to notice my heart racing all the time, even when I wasn't seeing someone in the clinic."

"That's not good. What did you do?"

"The next time I was in Shell, I stopped by the hospital to see Wally and told him all about it. He took an x-ray and got an EKG, and then sat me down and told me that he was writing a letter to the other missionaries in Makuma, forbidding me from being in charge of the clinic."

"Did it help?"

"That same day my heart stopped racing and I haven't had the problem since. Wally is such a dear man and a wonderful doctor."

The next day we began packing and making preparations to fly to Quito for GMU's annual conference. Joyce was so excited to be able to visit with the kids. I was excited, too, since Dale would be flying in toward the end of the conference. I was feeling much better about Dale now. For one thing, I could tell during Ruth's visit that there really was nothing between her and Dale. Also, when we got back from Kapawari, there were three letters from Dale waiting for me. The first one was dated the day after I left California. One small error in the way he had addressed them caused them to arrive in a roundabout way, delaying their delivery. It was obvious from what he wrote that he was still very much interested in me and really looking forward to his visit.

But, I had to admit, my feelings were a little ambivalent. What if he didn't like it? After all, Ruth went away convinced that, if missions were in her future, it for sure wouldn't be in the jungle. Worse yet, what if Dale said he liked it just so I would marry him? I had seen examples of couples where one of them felt called to the mission field and the other just tagged along. It didn't work well.

I remembered back to the day on my first trip to Ecuador when John, the three Shuar men and I arrived in Shell to wait for our flight into Yaapi. Lots of missionaries and others passed through Shell on their way into and out of the jungle. Those who lived in Shell were often responsible for feeding or housing the visitors. The evening we were there, we were assigned to a certain missionary's house for dinner. I arrived early to see if I could help the wife get dinner on the table. As we worked, I got an earful. This woman was very unhappy with her lot in life. She complained about the house they lived in, about how hard it was to keep the kids clean, about all the work involved in fixing a meal and about how her husband was never around to help. I was shocked, wondering why in the world this woman was here. I determined never to place myself in the position of dragging someone, kicking and screaming, down to the jungle.

There was a knock at the door. It was Tim Drown, Frank and Irene's son.

"Hi, Leslie. I just brought these over for you to give to Don, Bob and Ruthie when you see them."

He held open a plastic bag for me to see its contents. Inside was a living, crawling mass of inch-long flying ants.

"The Shuar told me they were starting to swarm, so I went and got some this morning. I knew the Stuck kids would want them."

"What for? I mean, what do you do with them?"

Tim looked at me with a puzzled expression. "You eat them," he answered matter-of-factly. Then, just to prove he wasn't making it up, he picked one out of the bag and popped it in his mouth. It made a crunching sound as he chewed.

"Just like that? Raw?" I asked.

"Well, some people prefer to fry them in a little butter."

"Oh, I see. Wings and all?"

"That's optional," Tim assured me. "You know, you can't argue with people's taste."

He turned to go. "Oh, almost forgot. The plane brought some mail this morning. Here's yours," he said as he held out a couple of envelopes. "Who's this Doctor Tivi?"

He might as well have handed me a live 220-volt wire. I just stood there, unable to answer him. Tim shrugged his shoulders, turned and walked off. I was left holding the explosive material.

Just like that, in seconds, all the emotions I had tried to suppress in the weeks since Kapawari came erupting out of my soul. I put a hand out to the doorframe then slid down to a seated position on the Shuar stool on the porch. It took a moment to work up my nerve to look at the envelope but when I did, sure enough, the return address said: Doctor Tivi, Epp Memorial Hospital, Shell, Pastaza. I tried to calm myself.

Well, what did I expect? After all, I did send him the quiver and darts as promised. It was only natural he would write a thank-you note letting me know he had received them. It didn't mean anything more than that.

A vivid memory came to mind of how I had struggled with whether or not to include my note with the quiver. I didn't want to appear too forward or anxious. Better to let him write to me first, if he was so inclined. But in the end I decided that, what the heck, I already had a boyfriend and I'd probably never even see this guy again, so why not? And now, here in my trembling hands, was my reward for being bold and taking a chance. I turned the envelope over and broke the seal. Inside was a single, neatly-folded sheet of unlined stationery. Fighting to maintain control, I opened the sheet and began reading the neat, but masculine handwriting.

"Dear Joyce and Leslie," it began. I stopped and re-read it, not believing what I was seeing. But it still said the same thing the second time I read it. I could feel my disappointment rising.

*I write a personal note to him and he answers 'Dear Joyce **and** Leslie'? What a creep! He doesn't even give me top billing.*

I was still stuck on the greeting, fuming, when Joyce bounded up the stairs.

"Hey, mail!" she called out. "Anything for me?"

"It's all for you," I pouted as I thrust it at her.

I regained my composure in time to hide my disappointment from Joyce. But I also resigned myself to the simple fact, now proven by this lame, impersonal note, that Kevin viewed me as nothing more than a friend. I set my will to the task of gathering any remaining hopes I harbored about Kevin's role in my life and shoving them out of my mind.

Chapter 23
Kevin's Confession

Receiving Leslie's note caused a change in my plans. She and Joyce were going to be in Quito for the week prior to my scheduled return flight to Tampa. It would be fun to see them one more time before I left. I consulted Wally and John, and they consented to my leaving Shell a week earlier than anticipated. It would work out well, in that I could accompany Lou on his journey back to Quito. I jotted a quick reply and delivered it to the mail bin at MAF, not at all certain that it would reach Makuma prior to their departure. The following Sunday, Lou and I boarded the bus en route to Quito.

The HCJB compound occupies a city block in Quito. The compound contains the offices, recording studios and broadcasting facilities of HCJB, the "Voice of the Andes". Standing on the compound looking west, one can see HCJB's repeater stations perched atop the towering peak of nearby Pichincha Mountain.

Across the street from the compound toward the south was HCJB's Rimmer Memorial Hospital. Next to it was the campus of Alliance Academy, a K-12 boarding school taught in English. Missionary kids from all over Latin America attend. At about midpoint of the street bordering the compound on its side opposite the hospital and school, a short street jutted off perpendicularly. The name of the street was Vozandes, but it was better known as "Missionary Row." One side of the street is dominated by three large buildings owned and occupied by GMU. The first is a square, brick building which houses GMU's offices. Next door is the dormitory for students whose parents live and work elsewhere. That is where the Stuck kids lived while attending the Alliance Academy. Finally, beyond the dorm is the guesthouse, a way-station for missionaries and others passing through Quito. On the opposite side of Missionary Row were a number of single family houses, most of which were occupied by HCJB missionaries. One of the houses closest to the radio compound was the home of Doug and Darlene Peters. I had made hasty arrangements to stay with them during this week in Quito.

It was late afternoon by the time I arrived. I had just enough time to drop my bags in the upstairs guest room and grab a quick snack before being whisked away to evening church service with the Peters family. English Fellowship Church was located a couple of blocks from their home. As we waited to cross busy *Avenida de las Americas,* I wished I had worn a sweater. I had forgotten how cool the evenings became at this altitude. There was a saying among the *Quitenos* that the city experienced all four seasons each day – starting with spring in the morning and ending with winter at night.

The church was near capacity when we arrived, but we were able to find seats together in a pew about halfway down the aisle. The place sounded more like a social club than a house of worship. I was used to a much more reverent atmosphere in the Catholic churches I had attended. Soon the service began with the singing of a hymn followed by some announcements. I was distracted from the announcements by a commotion at the rear of the church. All of a sudden, Joyce appeared, standing in the aisle at the end of our pew. She smiled and waved, then stepped back, revealing Leslie who appeared a bit embarrassed. She looked lovely, though. Joyce shoved Leslie down the pew in my direction. Leslie excused herself, stepping over people's feet down the length of the pew until she arrived where

I was seated. Room was made for her and she sat down without speaking. I nodded a greeting, and then pretended to pay attention to what was being said up front. In truth, though, I didn't hear a word of what was being said. All of the activity and the people around me, save one, faded from my consciousness. I was very aware of her presence, her breathing, her aroma. We stood to sing, sharing a hymnal, hands lightly touching. She noticed my ineptitude at finding a certain book of the Bible that the preacher referenced, assuaging my discomfort by inconspicuously indicating where it was located.

When the service ended I offered to walk Joyce and Leslie back to the GMU guesthouse where they were staying. As we stood talking in front of the guesthouse, Joyce said, "Kevin, you look like you're freezing. Let's go inside and talk."

Just to the right of the entryway was a small living room. It was simply but comfortably furnished with sofa and overstuffed chairs. Across the carpeted floor from the sofa was a fireplace. Joyce reached beneath the grate and pulled out an empty tuna can. She retrieved a container from around the corner of the fireplace and began to pour its contents into the can. I detected a familiar odor – gasoline. As Joyce retrieved a box of matches from the mantle and was preparing to light one, I stopped her.

"Are you nuts? You'll blow us all up."

She just laughed. "I know that's normally true, but at this altitude gasoline is much less flammable. It acts more like kerosene."

With that, she struck a match and touched it to the liquid in the shallow can. I flinched instinctively but, sure enough, the gasoline burned a slow, steady flame.

She placed the starter beneath the pre-positioned logs in the fireplace, stood and turned to me.

"I'm going to run along now," she began. "I want to go to the dorm to tuck the kids in. I've got some unpacking to do and a busy day in front of me tomorrow. It's the first day of our conference and I want to get out there for the opening session. There'll be a dinner in the evening. Would you be interested in joining us?"

"Sure," I replied. "What time?"

She thought for a moment. "I'll borrow a car and pick you up in front of the Peters' house at 5:30. The conference is at a retreat center about twenty minutes outside of the city. Now you two young people just enjoy yourselves."

Leslie, quiet to this point, began to object, but by that time Joyce was halfway up the stairs. There was an awkward moment of silence.

"Umm, the fire feels good." I was not comfortable having to be the one to initiate conversation.

Leslie ignored my feeble attempt at making conversation. She was jittery, on edge. After some time she turned to face me and said, "I was glad to see you in church tonight."

Relieved that the ice was breaking and the burden of carrying the conversation was being lifted from my shoulders, I smiled, "Yeah, I was really surprised when you came in. I didn't think you would arrive in Quito until tomorrow, so when I saw you I thought…"

She interrupted. "So, how long have you been a Christian?"

I was stunned. It was obvious that this girl had not mastered the art of light conversation. I tried to joke my way out of a tight spot.

"You're not much on small talk, are you?"

"Not when there are more important things to talk about. So?"

"So, what?" I feigned ignorance.

"You know what. When did you accept the Lord?"

She was not about to let me evade the issue. I felt conflicted inside. On the one hand, who did she think she was asking me a personal question like that; on the other, it was refreshing to have someone show such uninhibited interest in me. I decided to play along.

"Well, to be honest with you, I'm not what you would call a Christian."

Her countenance fell.

Chapter 24
Leslie's Disappointment

I struggled not to show the depth of my disappointment at hearing Kevin's words. I wasn't sure what to say. I couldn't understand it.

He seemed to fit in so naturally during our time in Kapawari. He prayed. We sang hymns together in the services there. Tonight we just came from the evening worship service at English Fellowship Church. And now he informs me he's not a Christian? Talk about mixed messages!

"So, what are you?" I blurted out.

"Well, I was raised Catholic. And, actually, I was very religious as a child. I was even an altar boy back in the days when the Mass was said in Latin."

"Okay, so you started out religious. Then what happened?"

"Then I went off to college and became an agnostic."

"At Notre Dame?"

"Yeah, ironic, isn't it? I remember sitting in 8th grade homeroom at Saint Anne's elementary school and Sister Mary Joseph telling us that some of us would 'lose the faith' when we went to college. Considering some of my classmates, I didn't think that was much of a stretch, but I knew it would never happen to me. At the time, I was seriously considering becoming a Trappist monk – you know, living in a monastery, vows of silence, the whole nine yards."

I was fascinated, yet apprehensive.

"Anyway, as a pre-med student at Notre Dame, I was taught to question everything and eventually got around to questioning if there was a God. I decided there was no way to prove it one way or the other, so I became an agnostic."

"I thought Notre Dame was real conservative."

"Well, it had been. I remember freshman year some of the upper classmen talking about how they had to wear a coat and tie to the dining hall for dinner. In fact, when I went there it was still an all-boys' school. Fortunately, they are beginning to wake up to the fact that the world is changing."

"But people haven't changed."

"Exactly my point. It's time people do change. Maybe then we could stop killing each other. Maybe if our leaders had more guts we could avoid disasters like Watergate or Vietnam."

"Sounds like you've been listening to campus radicals too much."

"Yeah, well, you may think it's radical for people to live together in peace, but not me."

"I see. So you believe all that 'Age of Aquarius' baloney."

"You can call it whatever you want, but the truth is that we'd be halfway there by now if it hadn't been for a few fascist nuts murdering our best leaders. If Martin Luther King and the Kennedy brothers were still alive right now, this would be a different world."

"Well, that's for sure."

"You can be sarcastic if you want, but it doesn't change the facts. Our entire society is corrupt, from the top down. All our leaders are hypocrites. They want to keep us down with a bunch of rules and regulations that they don't even follow themselves."

I didn't have a good feeling about where this conversation was heading, so I decided to try to change the direction.

"So, where does God fit into all of this?"

"God?" He raised his eyebrows. "God is the excuse the establishment uses to keep us all under their thumb. Pretty convenient, since nobody can see him."

"So you went to a Catholic school, but you don't believe in God? I thought they would at least make you take religion classes or something."

"Well, yeah, everybody has to take a couple of theology and philosophy courses." He paused. "Actually, it was one of my philosophy classes that really got me to thinking. We read a book by a guy named William James who calls himself a 'pragmatic philosopher'. His point is that what you believe is only important if it's going to make a difference in the way you act. If not, then who cares?"

"And you think that what you believe doesn't affect what you do?"

"Maybe for some people, but not for me. I think I can show Christian love without believing all the mumbo-jumbo."

"I see. So you think it's what you do that counts, rather than what you believe?"

"Of course. People can say whatever they want, but 'actions speak louder than words'. Believe me, I've known lots of people who call themselves Christians, but the way they act is like total hypocrites."

"But that's just the point. If you put your trust in people you'll always be disappointed. That's why you can only trust God."

"**If** there's a God," he hastened to correct me.

I decided to take another tack. I figured I needed to start with the very basics, something that was unarguable.

"Okay. So let me ask you this. Do you believe you're a sinner?"

"That depends on what you mean by 'sinner'.

I was floored. This was going to be harder than I thought.

He continued. "Sure, I'll admit I've done some things I probably shouldn't have, but nothing major. I mean, I never robbed a store or killed anybody. All in all, I'd say I'm on the positive side of the scale."

I couldn't believe the nerve of him. I wasn't about to let him go on, unopposed.

"But the Bible says, 'all have sinned and fall short of the glory of God'. That's why Christ came. That's why we need a savior. There's nothing we can do in ourselves to earn our way into heaven. It's totally a gift from God."

"'The Bible says, the Bible says'." There was a hint of irritation in his voice. "Can't you think for yourself?"

I struggled to keep my composure. I was determined not to let him make me upset, like he did in Kapawari.

"Have you ever read the Bible?" I asked in as meek a tone as I knew how.

"Yeah, a little."

I reached for one of many worn Bibles in the bookshelf next to the fireplace. Choosing one, I sat down on the couch in front of the fireplace and began paging through it.

"Come here. Let me show you what it says."

Without protest, he sat down right next to me. There was ever-so-slight contact between us. I found this very distracting but I couldn't very well object. He seemed genuinely interested. This was my chance. I flipped to a familiar passage.

"See, right here in the second chapter of Ephesians it says, 'For by grace you have been saved through faith; and that not of yourselves, it is the gift of God; not as a result of works, that no one should boast.' It couldn't be plainer. We're saved by what we believe, not by what we do."

"That's nice, **if** you believe the Bible."

"You're full of 'ifs'," I pointed out in exasperation. "Don't you believe in anything?"

He paused a moment.

"I believe I like sitting here next to you," he said. There was a sweet smile on his face, as he reached over to flick a stray strand of hair out of my face.

I jumped up. I was very uncomfortable. He was not at all interested in what I was saying. I was disappointed at the shallowness of his comment. I was not going to stick around for this.

"I don't know how serious you are about wanting to believe, but I know God is if you honestly seek Him. Anyway, I need to get to bed."

Without looking back I headed up stairs.

"Will I see you tomorrow?" he called out after me.

I pretended not to hear his question. The truth of the matter was that I was confused and uncertain whether or not I wanted to see him again. As I climbed the stairs, my mind was a whirl. As much as I hated to, I had to admit that Kevin did have a point. He really did act more like my idea of how a Christian should act than some of the guys I knew from Biola. But on the other hand, what blatant arrogance for him to think he wasn't a sinner.

As I entered the guest room that I shared with Joyce, she must have seen on my face the struggle taking place within me.

"Leslie, what's wrong? What is it?"

"Oh, Joyce. I found out Kevin's an agnostic. He doesn't even see himself as sinful. He doesn't believe the Bible and he sees no need for God in his life."

I could see by her face that Joyce shared my concern. But rather than get all upset, like I was, she just said, "Well, then we'd better pray for him."

And we did, for a long, long time. Still, I had a hard time sleeping that night. It wasn't just about Kevin's relationship with God, as important as I knew that was. But what did it all mean for me? I had to admit I liked being close to him. Yet, now that I knew he was not a Christian, I needed to be very careful. I needed to guard my heart.

Lord, why did You send Kevin my way at this point in my life? What is it You want me to learn from all this?

Chapter 25
Kevin Rebuffed

The following day Lou Hill and I hopped on one of the many municipal buses heading down *Avenida 10 de agosto* to old-town Quito. Lou had a fascination for ancient artifacts and, apparently, some knowledge of them. We snaked our way in and out of a myriad of shops with shelves full of small clay figurines. We were assured that all were authentic Incan artifacts, but Lou knew better. We continued the search until one of the shopkeepers relented and showed us his "special collection" in the rear of his store. To be honest, I couldn't see any difference between these and the dozens of others we had passed over earlier. Lou, however, was quite excited at this find and paid accordingly. While downtown, I purchased a coffee table-type book about Ecuador to give to the Peters for their many kindnesses to me.

Frankly, I didn't enjoy the time all that much. It should have been another fun adventure with Lou, but I couldn't stop thinking about my conversation with Leslie the night before. I wasn't accustomed to sharing my views with someone else, but she wasn't like anyone I had ever met. She just kept asking and asking. And it seemed like she was really interested in what I thought, even if she didn't agree with it. But now I was sorry I had opened up so much. It wasn't like me. I had always been an introvert, probably because of what I went through as a kid. As I sat there waiting for Lou to make up his mind about an armless statue, my mind drifted back to my early upbringing.

My otherwise happy childhood had been marred by a double curse. Not only was I fat, I was also smart. Now, it's easy enough to ignore a dumb, fat child or, better yet, adopt him into the peer group as a sort of mascot – a convenient target for cruel childhood humor. If the cherub were dumb enough he might not even recognize what was being done to him. And even if he did, the primal urge for social acceptance would win out over any need to maintain a sense of dignity.

Unfortunately, in my case it was impossible to humbly accept my assigned role in the social order of the playground. From my earliest school days, teachers held me up as an example of what could be accomplished by anyone willing to work hard and behave properly. This, of course, endeared me to my fellow students. The more I sought anonymity by minding my own business, the more I was thrust into the spotlight by my teachers.

A minor, but illustrative example of my predicament was provided by the recurring horror of the school play. Invariably, I was chosen for a lead role in the dreaded affair and, just as surely, disaster followed. It began as early as kindergarten. I was designated to play the lead role in a simple but compelling production in celebration of Columbus Day. Huddled with a group of fellow pilgrims on the deck of a plywood ship, all that was required of me was to shimmy up the wooden mast, shield my eyes from the sun as I gazed at the horizon and announce, "Land ho!" I practiced my line until I knew it forward and backward. The day before we were to perform in front of all the proud parents, we staged a dress rehearsal, complete with facade of a single-masted Spanish galleon. Right on cue, I climbed the mast – or, rather, tried to. There was no way my flabby arms were going to lift my pudgy lump of a body above the heads of my fellow explorers. Reluctantly, Mrs. Antwerp assigned my role to a more athletic classmate whose haughty look of vindication I will never forget.

Similar disasters followed in subsequent years culminating in the Great Christmas Humiliation of fifth grade. This was designed as a much larger production to be shown to the entire faculty, students and parents on the night before the start of Christmas break. Once again, my role was simple, yet profound. In a poignant scene I, as Joseph, was to enter from stage right and take up a position behind Mary who was kneeling before the Babe in the manger. That was it – a simple vignette – no speaking lines. I was so relieved. What could possibly go wrong? The big night arrived. I was resplendent in my long robe flowing from my fake beard to my borrowed, oversized sandals. On cue, I walked across the stage and entered the cramped wooden shed. There was Mary, kneeling to one side of the manger, gazing serenely at the Christ child. There wasn't enough room to pass behind Mary so I had to step over her kneeling legs. As I did, my sandal caught on the hem of my robe, throwing my weight off balance. With a desperate kick I freed my foot, but not before crashing ingloriously into the side of the shed. The audience erupted in laughter. Beet-red, I turned to face the audience, pretending that nothing unscripted had happened. As the laughter faded, I began to regain my composure. Out of the corner of my right eye I could see that the picture of a donkey head, which had been thumb-tacked to the back of the shed to add realism to the scene, was still swaying back-and-forth. Suddenly, the donkey head dropped out of view. The resulting uproar echoed in my brain, confirming my ruined life and utter failure as a member of the human race.

My parents searched for me at the conclusion of the production. When I failed to appear at the snack table set up in the foyer, my mother knew something was terribly wrong. Her desperate search ended when she found me lying on the back seat of the family station wagon, sobbing. Her assurances that my performance was the highlight of an otherwise dull evening failed to provide the intended comfort.

To my good fortune obesity proved to be a temporary childhood affliction. Something magical happened to my body during the summer between seventh and eighth grade. As usual, I was oblivious to the changes occurring in my body as well as in my life. It awaited others to inform me and they soon obliged. It occurred while walking down the hallway on the first day of school following summer vacation.

As I passed a gaggle of girls, one of them cooed, "Hi, Kevin. How was your summer?"

Startled, I turned around to make sure she was talking to me. There was no one else there by that name. Embarrassed, I mumbled an unintelligible answer and hurried away as the girls giggled and chattered.

That day signaled a change in my life. My popularity with girls rose along with my height. Still, despite the fact that my baby fat melted away to reveal a masculine physique, no comparable change was happening inside. Although I tried to project a confident air to match my transformed physical appearance, on the inside I remained a shy little fat boy.

That evening Joyce picked me up as planned. I was disappointed that she came alone. We drove north out of the city and came to a picturesque old hacienda, El Inca. We arrived just in time for dinner. I could see Leslie across the room talking in an animated manner with a group of people. Joyce introduced me to other conference participants who were sitting at our table. As we took our places, Joyce made certain to seat Leslie and me next to one another. It did not have its desired effect. Leslie was cordial to me but spent most of the meal talking to the person on her other side about his orchid collection. Leslie's dad was some kind of horticulturalist or something, so she was acting very interested. It sounded pretty boring to me, so I stayed out of it.

At a rare break in their conversation, I spoke up. "I talked to Don and Bob at the dorm today and they said I could borrow their bikes tomorrow to ride to the Equator Monument. Would you like to come?"

"That's very nice of you, but I'll be here at the conference all day."

"Oh, okay." I resigned myself to going alone.

Joyce overheard our conversation and interjected. "That sounds like so much fun. Leslie, you've just got to go."

"But, Joyce, the conference…"

"Well, you're not a GMU missionary, so you don't have to go. Besides, it'll probably be pretty boring tomorrow. It's just all business stuff." Joyce caught herself and looked around to see if any of the mission leaders were within earshot and then continued in a lower voice, "If I had the choice between riding bikes to the equator and sitting through business meetings, I know what I'd do. You just plan on going. I'll cover for you here."

That was that, and the conversation moved on. When dinner was ended I made arrangements with Leslie for the following day, bid goodbye to those at the table and walked outside with Joyce.

Before we even reached the car, she struck. "Leslie told me about your conversation last night. I mean about being an agnostic and all."

"Yeah. I just don't see how you could ever prove that God exists."

Frankly, I was getting kind of sick of talking about it. I considered for a moment, and then decided to unload with both barrels.

"Besides, there are so many different religions, why would anyone believe one rather than another? And does that mean everybody else is going to hell?"

It was supposed to be a rhetorical question, but Joyce answered, "I know what you mean, but the thing about Christianity that makes it so much different than all the others for me is the fact that every other religion is based on some formula for earning your way into heaven. Christianity just admits no one can do that, and so we all need to rely on what Jesus has already done for us." She paused. "Do you believe Jesus lived here on earth?"

"Well, sure. I mean, we have pretty good proof from history books other than just the Bible."

"Good. That's a start." She seemed relieved. "But what do you believe about Him? Who was He? What was He doing here?"

"I think he was a good man and moral teacher – like Mahatma Ghandi."

"I see. The only problem with that is that Jesus would disagree with you. He claimed to be God. That's blasphemy. That's why the people wanted to kill Him. So He can't be a good, moral man and a blasphemer all at the same time. Either He's right about being God, or else He's some kind of nut."

I saw an opportunity to put the pressure back on her. "Alright, then, what makes you think he's not a kook? How can you prove he's God?"

Joyce was silent. I wondered if I had gone too far in attacking her beliefs. I began to feel bad. After all, she had been nice enough to invite me out here to dinner. I was about to apologize when she said, "Kevin, you ask some pretty deep theological questions. I'm not a theologian, and I don't feel very adequate to answer them for you. All I do know is what Christ has done in my life and what I've seen him do in the lives of others. I don't think the changes I've seen can be explained unless what the Bible says about Jesus is true."

By that time we had reached the car. The conversation changed as we drove home, but I couldn't stop thinking about what Joyce had said. The thing that struck me was how similar it was to something else I heard before. It happened back at Notre Dame when I first began questioning everything. The rector of Dillon Hall, where I lived, was Father Jim Burtchaell. Father Jim had an impressive intellect. Already, as a young man, he was Dean of Theology at Notre Dame. I remembered one night sitting around in a dorm room with a group of students, peppering Father Jim with the same sort of questions I was asking Joyce. After forty-five minutes of graciously enduring our sophomoric inquisition, Father Jim said, "Gentlemen, if you're asking me to prove scientifically that God exists, I can't do it – nor do I know anyone who can. When it comes right down to it, the reason I believe in God is because I can't deny the way I've seen God work in men's lives."

It all sounded rather unscientific to me, but now here was the second person I respected saying basically the same thing.

Could they be right?

Chapter 26
Leslie Lightens Up

The next morning Kevin stopped by the GMU guest house to pick me up. In spite of the early hour, I was ready when he arrived. That was unusual for me, since it usually takes me a while to get going in the morning. But, again, I had spent a restless night, concerned for Kevin's lack of faith, and also wrestling with the growing attraction I felt for him. As much as I tried to set it aside, it just wouldn't go away. I loved the way he would focus his attention on me, yet at the same time remain aware of others and their needs. He always seemed to handle himself with confidence. This morning he greeted me with a warm smile.

"Hi, Sunshine. Looks like we've got a perfect day brewing for a bike ride." Then, in a lower, softer voice, he continued, "I'm really glad you decided to join me."

A bit flustered at his intimate tone of voice, I began to introduce him to the woman who ran the guest house, but then caught myself.

"Oh, you two must already know one another."

It was obvious from the looks on their faces that they did not. I turned to Kevin.

"I thought you stayed here on your way to Shell."

"I did, but I came in late at night and left early the next morning."

"I see. Well, Kevin, this is Barb Youderian. Barb, this is Kevin."

They chatted for just a moment and then we left.

"Youderian?" Kevin asked when we were alone, "Wasn't that the name of one of the five missionaries killed by the Aucas?"

"Yes. Roger Youderian was Barb's husband."

Kevin appeared pensive.

"What?" I asked. "What are you thinking?"

"Oh, nothing really. It's just that here's another woman so committed that she returns to Ecuador as a widow with children to raise. If these people are wrong about what they believe, they sure are wasting their lives."

I couldn't resist the opening.

"Well, of course I doubt that what they believe plays any part in what they do."

He was quick to pick up my meaning.

"All right, that's enough out of you. We're not going to have any more of that kind of talk. Today is just for fun."

The day was spectacular – cloudless skies and, once we escaped the diesel fumes of the city, clean mountain air. The brisk temperature was ideal for bike riding. From the northern edge of the city, past the airport, it was downhill most of the way. There were long stretches where we didn't have to pedal at all. It was perfect – not a care in the world. About midway there we stopped at a little café perched on the mountainside. Kevin ordered a couple of Cokes, served warm the Ecuadorian way. We sat at a table to talk. I made sure to keep the conversation light. We used the opportunity to learn more about each other's families. He came from a big, close-knit family. He told me about his three brothers and three sisters and about family vacations and lots of sports activities they did together. Like me, he had had to move all the time as a child, since his dad was in the military.

"That reminds me," he said. "Didn't you mention in Kapawari that your dad was in the Marines, too?"

"Yep, he was a pilot. But then he was grounded when doctors discovered that he had a disease of his cornea that interfered with his vision. He's actually looking into getting a corneal transplant. It was hard for him to give up flying. He really loved it."

"So, what's he doing now?"

"He's a sales representative for a wholesale nursery. He has this van that he fills with plants and drives all over Orange County visiting his customers. He has to get up at 4 AM every day to beat the traffic."

"I don't think I could ever be a sales person."

"Dad doesn't seem to mind. It combines two things he loves: plants and people."

"And how about you? What do you love?"

"Well, it's a cinch it's not plants." I laughed. "As I was growing up, Dad would make me work in the yard. All my friends would be going to the beach or something fun, and I had to stay at home, baking topsoil in the oven."

"Baking topsoil?"

"Don't ask."

"Oh well, at least you learned a useful trade in case you come down with an eye disease."

"Well, actually, I do have the same disease as Dad. It runs in the family. His mom had it too"

"What? That's terrible. You're not going to need a corneal transplant or something, are you?"

The concern in his voice was very touching.

"I don't know. They found it in my eyes about ten years ago. So far it hasn't caused any major problems, but who knows?" I said, trying to appear blasé about the whole thing.

"It would be a crime to mess up those big, beautiful eyes of yours," he began, and then stopped. There was a moment of awkward silence.

I spoke up to rescue him from embarrassment. "Well, thank you. Actually, I used to get teased about my eyes when I was growing up. The boys in my class would shout 'What big eyes you have,' until I'd run away crying."

"Boys will be boys. I imagine they'd sing a different tune if they saw you today."

"I don't know about that. They made fun of me for having dark eyebrows with blonde hair, too. Kids can be so cruel."

"Tell me about it. I was a fat little kid in junior high. Guys used to make jokes about me all the time."

"You? Fat? Well, I guess you got the last laugh on them."

I felt like we were getting to know one another as real people. I began to feel at ease.

The cafe was swarming with flies. As we sipped our Cokes and chatted, Kevin casually disposed of a number of them with his bare hands. I was impressed. At one point he even squashed two of them on the table top with a single blow.

"How'd you do that?" I asked.

"It's really nothing. One summer, I was a lifeguard at a motel pool. The place was covered with flies. If it weren't for them, I would have been very lonely. Almost no one used the pool the whole summer. With all the flies and time to kill, I was able to perfect my technique."

"Which is …?"

"Sorry, it's a trade secret."

I smacked him on the arm in a playful sort of way.

"All right, all right. Now watch. When a fly lands, you slowly bring your hand about six inches over him."

He was demonstrating the technique at the same time he was narrating.

"Right then, the fly has to decide if it's a threat or not. If he thinks it is, he'll fly off and you won't get him. But if he doesn't fly off he'll sit there thinking about it, sometimes for quite a while. If you hold your hand real steady, eventually he'll think your hand is just part of the environment. Now's the crucial time. Wait for him to start moving his little hands, cleaning his eyes or his wings, not paying attention to you and then…"

Whack! He lifted his hand to show me the crushed carcass.

"If you're patient, you'll almost never miss."

We continued on our way, arriving at the equator in early afternoon. There was a monument marking the exact location of the equator – a sort of chopped-off obelisk with a globe on top. It had a line running through it and down the sidewalk on either side, so that you could stand with one foot in each hemisphere. At one point we sat in the shade of a eucalyptus tree on the side of a berm. It was such a perfect day and we were having such easy conversation that I began to wonder again if, perhaps, there was some potential in this relationship. I had to remind myself that there was no way we could be anything more than friends.

"This has been a lot of fun, but I think we'd better start back if we hope to make it to Quito before dark," he suggested.

He offered me his hand to help me up the incline. I accepted the offer, but when we reached the top of the rise I pulled my hand away. I needed to be very careful. I had never been so attracted to a guy before in my life. But without sharing the same faith, our relationship could go nowhere. I didn't want to send him any mixed messages. I knew I had no business getting involved with him. After all, I already had a boyfriend. What would Kevin think, knowing I had a boyfriend, if I held his hand the way that I wanted to?

We started pedaling back to Quito and soon came to regret all the coasting we had done on the way out. We encountered hill after hill, each one seemed to be steeper and longer than the one before. As the afternoon wore on, I became concerned that we were not going to make it back before nightfall. In the mountains on the equator the sun sets fast. Dusk is fleeting.

I was tiring. Whether from the strenuous exertion or due to the thin mountain air, I found my breaths coming in short gasps. Kevin kept encouraging me to "make one more hill – you can do it." I was amazed at his stamina. With previous boyfriends I had taken pride in outperforming them in feats of endurance. Here I was struggling just to keep up with Kevin, whose pedaling seemed almost effortless. I was resigning myself to the inevitability of having to dodge traffic in the dark when another problem arose. Out of nowhere, black, threatening clouds appeared. The wind rose, the temperature dropped, and we could see sheets of rain coming down in the distance.

"We're not going to make it!" I shouted to Kevin, who nodded in agreement.

As the first fat drops began to splat on us, he dismounted his bike, turned around and stuck out his thumb.

"Stick with me. I've had lots of experience hitchhiking. Once I hitched all the way from Notre Dame to Seattle and then back to Washington, D. C."

Experience paid off. The very next vehicle to come along pulled over and stopped. It was a small, dilapidated red pickup truck. An older man and his son were seated on the bench seat in the cab. The son rolled down the window.

"A donde?" the old man inquired.

"A Quito," Kevin replied.

The old man motioned to throw the bikes in the bed of the truck as the son scooted over. There was just enough room for one more passenger.

"I can ride in the back with the bikes," Kevin offered.

I had the feeling from the way he said it that he was hoping I would insist that we ride together in the cab with me on his lap. I didn't fall for it. I took him up on his offer.

"Okay, but I hope you don't get wet back there."

He had about as much chance of staying dry as Noah. To make matters worse, the rain soon turned to hail. The clatter on the roof made it impossible to hear the old man, who maintained a nonstop stream of conversation in Spanish. All of a sudden, I was gripped by panic. This might have been a very foolish decision.

What if these men drove us to a destination of their own choosing? What if they had picked us up in order to take advantage of me?

I now regretted my decision to not insist that Kevin join me in the truck's cab. I would feel so much safer with him next to me. Yet, even as I acknowledged the fact, I scolded myself.

I'm perfectly capable of taking care of myself.

Still, it would have been nice to have him there beside me.

We arrived in Quito just before nightfall. The kind old man went out of his way to drop us off right in front of the GMU dorm. I felt ashamed of the fears and suspicions I had experienced. Kevin was soaked to the skin and freezing. I felt so bad for him. After putting the bikes away, he crossed the street to the shelter of the Peters' house.

Chapter 27
Kevin Trapped

The following afternoon I telephoned Leslie at the guest house when she returned from El Inca.

"Hi," I began, "how was the conference?"

"Uh, good." I noticed a hesitation in her voice.

"Listen, the reason I'm calling is that several of us have made arrangements to go out to dinner at the Hotel Quito tomorrow night, and I was wondering if you would be interested in joining us. So far, it's the Swansons, Sara Risser and I. What do you think?"

"That sounds nice. Actually, I'm really glad you called. See, I was going to invite you out to get some dessert with me."

This was an unexpected surprise. "Really? When?"

"How about tonight?"

"Are you serious? Tonight?"

"Yeah, I know it's kind of short notice but..." She paused as if considering what to say next.

"To be honest with you, Joyce made arrangements for you to have dessert with some people named the Adams and then suggested that I ask you. You don't have to go if you don't want to."

"Oh?" I was interested, but suspicious. "And who, exactly, are the Adams?"

"Well, Tom Adams is an American businessman here in Quito. He and his wife go to English Fellowship Church. I guess Joyce was talking to some people at the conference about you, and they suggested Joyce get you together with Tom, since he comes from a similar background as you."

"A similar background, meaning…?"

"You know, like scientific."

"This is beginning to sound like a trap."

"No, nothing like that. Joyce just thought you might like talking with him."

"Um-hmm." Dead silence.

"Okay, look, I'll make you a deal," she offered. "I'll go with you tomorrow night, if you'll come with me tonight."

"You're on. What time should I come by for you?"

"They're expecting us at 7:00, so how about 6:30?"

"'They're expecting us'?" I asked.

"Well, I mean, **if** we're coming."

"Hmm, I see. All right, then. See you at 6:30."

At 6:30 we hailed one of Quito's ubiquitous taxis and handed the driver a slip of paper with the address that Joyce had written on it. We entered a well-to-do neighborhood full of large, neat, attractive homes. Each was surrounded by lush gardens and protected by eight-foot high walls of white-painted plaster topped with broken glass. At the house our taxi cab driver indicated, we were admitted through the outer gate by the uniformed Ecuadorian guard and greeted by Tom and Judy Adams at the front door. They were an attractive couple, appearing to be in their late-forties or early-fifties. He was tall and thin, dressed in coat and tie. She was petite and quite gregarious.

"Come in, come in," she insisted. "We've heard **so** much about you."

Yeah, I'll bet.

Soon, she was off to the kitchen to make coffee, leaving Tom and me in the drawing room playing pool with Leslie watching. I had played my fair share of pool in college, but you would never know it by my performance that night. I wanted to tell Leslie, "I'm usually a lot better than this; I'm just nervous tonight," but what would be the use? She'd already witnessed my athletic prowess at soccer. Oh, well.

To my relief, Judy soon called us into the living room where she served a delicious *babaco* crisp with plenty of strong Ecuadorian coffee. *Babaco* is a star-shaped tropical fruit about the size of an elongated cantaloupe and color of an avocado. When properly prepared as a filling, its taste and texture was remarkably similar to apple. The conversation, as we enjoyed our dessert, was easy and free-flowing. Before long I began to loosen up.

"More coffee?" purred Judy.

"Don't mind if I do," I replied. "This coffee is delicious. Do you buy it here?"

"Yes, it's called *Sello Dorado*. It's actually grown in Colombia, but they sell it here in the market."

"Excellent," I exclaimed, holding out my cup for Judy to fill again.

My sense of comfort was short-lived. There were two contributing factors. For one, the conversation made its way around to "more serious" subjects. Unexpectedly, the previously taciturn Tom launched into a rather prolonged and impassioned description of his spiritual journey as a young man. I began to squirm, though not so much in response to what he was saying. I was becoming used to such overtures. No, the second and overriding reason for my discomfiture had to do with the amount of coffee I had been consuming during the course of the evening. What began as a mild sensation of fullness at the beginning of his discourse soon blossomed into a full-blown sense of panic. I felt as though someone was inflating my bladder with a bicycle pump, it progressed so rapidly. I crossed and re-crossed my legs. A cold sweat broke out on my forehead. I had trouble following the conversation. In any normal situation I would have asked to be excused, but how could I politely do that now, with Tom pouring out his soul to me? I set my will to endure to the end. Once or twice I doubted I would make it. I was aware of conversation going on about me, but oblivious to what was being said. Everything was a blur. Finally, as if from another room, words entered my consciousness.

"So, what do you think?" Tom asked.

I looked up to see all eyes riveted on me.

"Do you have any questions?" chimed in Judy.

"Yes," I blurted out, "could I use your bathroom?"

By the time I came out, Leslie had her sweater on, standing with the Adams by the front door, conversing in low tones. Although everyone was very pleasant, I could sense the disappointment in all of them. Just beneath the veneer of polite conversation was the implied question: "So, **this** is the deep thinker you wanted us to talk to?"

Chapter 28
Leslie's Confusion

I felt time and opportunity slipping away. Last night's well-intentioned but fruitless visit with the Adams had been disastrous. Now here we were sharing an awkward moment of silence while seated on the couch in the GMU guesthouse.

The evening had been pleasant enough up until now. The Swansons had picked up Kevin and me first, and then Sara, and we all drove together to the Hotel Quito. I wished I had something more stylish to wear. I had purposely brought my out-of-date, longer dresses to Ecuador, thinking I would leave them with Joyce to distribute to those in need. Now here I was out to dinner with a doctor and his wife, the Director of HCJB's Health Care, and a medical student, in whom I was increasingly interested, at one of Quito's nicest restaurants. What was I doing in such distinguished company? I felt a bit intimidated. The restaurant was located on the top floor of the hotel with a commanding view of the city lights. The dinner was delicious and the company enjoyable. Charlotte Swanson made certain there was no lack of interesting conversation.

After dinner, while the others remained at the table sipping coffee, Kevin asked if I would like to join him out on the balcony to better appreciate the view. The hotel was built at the edge of a precipice, looking down on the Pifo valley to the east. It was a cold, clear, starry night. Kevin stood just behind me, closer than he should have. I could feel his breath on my hair. I fought the impulse to lean back against him.

"What an incredible view!" he whispered.

I nodded. "It's so beautiful."

I spoke without looking at him, drinking in the pleasant sensation of his nearness. I had never felt this way before. It felt so right ... until I remembered Dale. He would be arriving tomorrow. My excitement about his visit had grown cold. I felt guilty. How could I be feeling the way I was about Kevin — someone who was not a Christian? I knew I could never marry him if we didn't share the same faith. But at the same time, I couldn't deny that I admired him, enjoyed his company, felt proud to be with him. With other guys I had dated, there would often be something they said or did that made me cringe. But Kevin instinctively would say the words or do the thing that I expected and in the way I expected it. I was never disappointed. He was a perfect combination of the qualities I had admired in previous boyfriends, with none of the shortcomings. His kindness and compassion surpassed that displayed by many of my Christian friends. How could a nonbeliever exhibit such Christ-like behavior? It was all so confusing. I needed time to think, to sort it all out.

When the Swansons dropped us off in front of the guest house, I invited Kevin in. He didn't hesitate to accept the offer. Once again, we had the place to ourselves. All the guests had turned in for the night. We sat on the couch and talked and talked about everything and about nothing. Time seemed to stand still.

But now, the conversation had ground to a halt. I was trying to figure out how to say what I was feeling, what I wanted him to know.

The clock on the mantle chimed three.

"Holy mackerel! I better get out of here and let you get to bed!" he said. "I had no idea it was this late."

I made no effort to move. I turned my face away from him, so that he wouldn't be able to read my thoughts. This would be our last night together. I felt like I needed to say something to him to indicate the way I was feeling. The trouble was, I wasn't sure how I was feeling. In many ways, I was grateful for the character traits I had seen in him, even if our relationship could go no further. It gave me hope that there was a man out there somewhere who would satisfy the longing in my soul. Frantically, I searched for the right combination of words to express what was in my heart. My mind was blank. Feeling very self-conscious, I whispered:

"Kevin, I just want to thank you for showing me what I want in a man."

As soon as the words were out, I wanted to gather them all back in.

What an idiot. What is he going to think of me, saying something so stupid?

I wanted to disappear. I had no idea what he was thinking, because he just sat there, not saying a word, not moving a muscle. I was mortified.

He must hate me. He probably thinks I'm desperate to say something like that.

I was just about ready to jump up and run away when it happened. Without saying a word, he slid over on the couch, closing the distance between us. He tenderly placed his hand on my far shoulder and pulled my body against his. With his other hand he reached over, lifting my chin. I looked at his face bending closer to mine. He was going to kiss me! My mind was in total confusion. At the last second I turned away.

"No, please don't." I begged.

"Why not? What's wrong?"

"I'm afraid I'm falling in love with you."

"Good. There's nothing wrong with that."

"No, it just... it could never work." I hoped my words had the sound of finality that I wanted to convey.

I didn't dare kiss him. I knew I had to protect myself from the strong emotions I was already feeling.

He sat there as though stunned.

"So then, what did you mean by saying that I've shown you what you're looking for in a man?"

At last I felt an opportunity to try to explain the turmoil in my heart.

"Do you remember my telling you in Kapawari that there was a guy who wanted to marry me? Well, Dale's a wonderful Christian man and I respect him a lot, but he's not interested in missions. For years I've felt that the Lord was calling me to the mission field, and I really want to go – but I'd also like to get married. I've been so confused. One night in Makuma I finally just prayed, 'Lord, I can't take this anymore. If You really want me to serve You on the mission field, You're going to have to show me that I'm not supposed to marry Dale'. A couple of weeks later I met you. Right away I could see you had the same heart for the people as I do. I know I can't marry you if you're not a Christian, but at least now I see that there are men who feel the same way I do."

For a very long time he didn't answer. It seemed like he was wrestling with something inside. At last, he said:

"Leslie, there's something that I think you need to know. When I came down here I wasn't all that thrilled that it was a mission hospital I was coming to. I didn't feel like I needed or wanted that. But after living here with the missionaries in Shell, I've realized that there is something that's been missing in my life. At first I tried to ignore it, or explain it away, but I can't."

"But then how come you just keep arguing with Joyce and me every time we talk to you about it?"

"Partly because I like seeing if I can get under your skin," he smiled with a twinkle in his eye.

"You've done a pretty good job of that," I admitted.

"But, too, I think it's because I want to keep testing people to see if they really believe what they're saying. I admire the people I've met here for what they do. Frankly, I think any one of them would have been happy to trade places with the guys who were martyred."

"Yeah, I've wondered sometimes if I would be willing to die for my beliefs."

"And?"

"I don't know. I hope so, but I don't think you ever really know until it happens. What about you?"

"I have thought about it. And I agree there's no way to know for sure. It would be hard, but in some ways I think dying for your faith would be easier than living for your faith."

"What do you mean?"

"Well, martyrdom requires a one-time decision – all or nothing. But to live for your faith means making little decisions day after day to give up your life."

I was amazed by his depth of understanding.

He went on. "Anyhow, either way I want that sense of purpose in my life. I've just been reluctant to buy the whole package they're selling. I've been trying to get somebody to admit that they could do what they're doing without God in the picture."

"Any luck?"

"No," he admitted. "As much as I've fought it, I've come to the realization that, apart from a relationship with God, people are pretty much looking out for their own interests. And deep down I'm just as selfish as anybody else."

"That's exactly why you need to accept Christ as your savior. That's what I've been trying to tell you."

"I know. I know. I've come to accept that. The problem is, I don't want to do it here."

I was confused. "What do you mean? Why not?"

"Because my whole life I've struggled with peer pressure, with wanting to please other people. So the easiest thing in this case would be for me to just say 'Sure, I believe'. Then everybody would be happy and leave me alone. But this is too important a decision to do that with. I mean, think about it – here I am in very unusual surroundings with a bunch of weird people. What if, when I got back to my normal life, I decided this all just seemed like a dream or something? I don't want that. I figure if God is real, he'll be real back in Florida, same as he is here."

"But what if your plane crashes on the way back to Florida?"

"Don't you think God's in control of that?"

I couldn't tell for sure if he was baiting me again or not, so I just let it pass. Maybe I should have pressed harder for him to make a decision right then, but I didn't.

"Just make sure you don't wait too long," I pleaded.

I felt very tired. This was all too much for me. I needed time to sort through all of this and figure it out.

"Well, maybe I had better get to bed," I said. "I'm supposed to pick up Dale at the airport in a couple of hours."

"What?! He's coming here?"

"Yeah, didn't I tell you? I invited him down so he could see what the mission field was like."

"Uh, no. You forgot to mention that to me."

I could tell Kevin was dumbfounded, but then again, so was I. I wouldn't have had the energy to explain anything to him, even if I had understood it myself. I felt like I was sleepwalking as I climbed the stairs and entered the room I was sharing with Joyce.

Very quietly I turned the knob and pushed open the door, so as not to awaken her. Tiptoeing across the room to the closet where my nightgown was hanging, my step caused one of the floorboards to creak. Joyce shot up in bed.

"Well? Well? Did he accept the Lord?" She blurted out as she fumbled for the lamp switch.

"No, Joyce, but I think he's close."

I was assaulted by a confusing array of competing emotions. Afraid to let Joyce see in my face and the battle going on inside of me, I turned away.

Joyce was alerted. Perhaps it was my body language or something in my tone of voice. Whatever it was, Joyce had to explore it.

"Leslie, is there something going on between you and Kevin?"

I just couldn't contain the swirling crosscurrents of thoughts and emotions churning inside of me. Filled with guilt for the way I was feeling on the one hand, and the elation of the memory of his embrace, the intimacy of our conversation on the other, I was weary of resisting the competing strains. Finally, the dam broke. I began a tentative confession in a weak, quavering voice. Tears welled up in my eyes.

"Oh, Joyce, I'm afraid I'm falling in love with him."

Even as I heard the words spoken aloud, I was embarrassed that they had come from my mouth. I knew that what I was feeling was wrong. How could I have allowed myself to fall into such a trap? If it had been one of my friends confessing such a thing to me, I would have set them straight in no uncertain terms. Yet, instead, it was me having to admit my weakness.

How humiliating! I braced myself for the lecture that I knew was coming and which, to my shame, was richly deserved.

"Oh, Leslie, that's wonderful!" Joyce exclaimed, as she clasped her hands together.

I was stunned. I stood there speechless, tears streaming down my face as she babbled on.

"Just think! You two can get married and come back here to Ecuador. He can be the doctor and you can be the nurse. It will be wonderful! Not that it **has** to be Ecuador. I mean, I'm sure God could use you two somewhere else if that's what you decide, but…"

My mind was reeling. I couldn't believe what I was hearing. Did she understand the situation? Had she been paying attention at all? I recovered my senses and interrupted.

"Joyce, what are you saying? I can't marry him. He's not even a Christian."

"Oh, I know that," replied Joyce in a dismissive tone of voice, "but he's going to accept the Lord. I just know he will."

The way she said it was as though that were the end of the discussion and nothing further need be said about. But I knew better.

"Joyce, slow down. Think about what you're saying. You and I have both seen relationships where the guy comes to know the Lord after he's met the woman. Almost always, she ends up as the spiritual leader in the relationship. That doesn't work well, and it's not what I want."

"Leslie, of course I know that; but this is different. You've seen Kevin. You know that his heart's sincere. And he's so smart, he'll learn things very fast and be the leader in the relationship – no problem."

"Well, I have to admit you're right about him being sincere. And he is smart; he doesn't miss much. But, Joyce, I just don't know about this."

"Yeah, you're right. I don't know all the answers either. But I know Someone who does. Let's pray for Kevin right now."

As we prayed, we pleaded with God that He would work in Kevin's heart and mind in such a way that Kevin would recognize his need for a relationship with Christ. We thanked God for the way that He had already been answering my desperate cry for guidance, and begged Him to continue to show me in no uncertain terms what He desired for my life.

By the time we finished praying, I felt the tide of battle beginning to turn in my heart. I still had serious misgivings, but I also felt a ray of hope that maybe, just maybe, God was planning something wonderful and out-of-the-ordinary in my life. Could it be? I wanted it so much that it scared me. I tried fighting it, but it was like trying to resist the current of the Kapawari River. And, just like in Kapawari, I felt as though it was all I could do to get my head above water for that next gulp of air.

Joyce's scheming mind was racing ahead.

"You've just got to see him again," she said.

Roused from my internal struggles, I exclaimed, "Joyce, are you crazy? I'd love to see Kevin again, but there's no way. I'm supposed to pick up Dale at the airport in two hours. Remember?"

"Yeah, I know." Joyce's voice was calm but resolute, like a general planning the next day's battle. "And then you two leave for Cuenca on Saturday, so it will have to be tomorrow – or rather today, I should say," she noted, glancing at the clock.

"Today? But... so, what am I supposed to do with Dale?"

"I'm not sure yet, but we'll figure something out. Right now, though, you had better get your beauty sleep, young lady."

With that, I crawled under the covers. Joyce switched off the lamp. We both lay wide awake in the dark, each not daring to talk so as not to disturb the other.

Chapter 29
Kevin Called Out

I slept until mid-morning and, by the time I got downstairs, the breakfast dishes were long since washed and put away.

"Late night?" Doug asked with an impish grin.

"Yeah, it was, kind of." I admitted.

I felt like I was hung over from the night before. My head was still reeling from all that had happened. It was a baffling situation. Was Leslie interested in continuing some kind of relationship with me or not? Everything had been left so up-in-the-air. I realized I didn't really know whether or not we would ever see or talk to each other again. Where was I supposed to go from here?

The Peters' daughter, Debbie, was in the living room practicing piano. The melancholic strains of Beethoven's *Fur Elise* expressed well my sense of romantic loss. My wallowing self-pity was short-lived, however, interrupted by a knock on the door.

Doug came back from answering the knock. "It's Joyce Stuck. She wants to talk to you."

Surprised, I went to the foyer and could see Joyce through the still-open front door. She had backed down off the stoop and was standing in the middle of the short walk leading from the street. She looked nervous.

"Hi, Joyce," I called out, not wanting to give any hint of what had been taking place between me and her young ward. "I didn't expect to see you today."

Joyce came right to the point. "Kevin, you have got to see Leslie today." The way she said it made it sound like a challenge, like a football coach's half-time speech to his losing team.

"What are you talking about, Joyce?" I asked. "Her boyfriend just arrived. They're practically engaged."

"I know, I know, but you still need to see her."

"No way. That's out of the question." I was resolute.

"But you're interested in her, aren't you?"

"Well, yes, but it just wouldn't be right."

"Wouldn't be right?" She was no longer able to contain her emotions. "Wouldn't be right?" Then, with a defiant look, "Are you a man or a mouse?"

I was floored. Here was this nice religious lady calling my manhood into question because I was trying to do the honorable thing. Life was not making sense. I stood there speechless.

"Leslie wants to see you."

"She does?" Now she was getting my attention.

"Yes, she does. So how about if she comes by here tonight?"

"Well, okay. I guess so. What time?"

"I'm not really sure. It depends."

I was getting the sense that this was going to be a covert operation.

"Hmm, I see. Well, I don't have any plans for tonight, so I'll be here if she wants to drop by."

I figured by leaving the initiative with her I'd protect myself from being accused of stabbing her boyfriend in the back.

"Great. I'll let her know you're expecting her," Joyce ended and hurried away.

That evening after dinner, Darlene suggested a game of Scrabble so she, Doug, David and I played. I was trying to figure out how to work my "Q" onto a triple letter score block, when there was a knock on the door. Darlene got up to see who was there and came back with a sheepish-looking Leslie following behind.

I realized that if this relationship stood any chance of getting off the ground I for sure did not want it to start off with Leslie thinking I was at her beck and call. So, after everyone greeted one another, I invited her to have a seat while the Peters and I finished the game. Before long, Darlene went out with a 16-point word to win the game. I suggested to Leslie that we take a walk. We excused ourselves and headed out the door into the damp, cold night.

We no sooner reached the street then Leslie turned to me and said, "So, what did you want to talk to me about?"

I sensed some trickery afoot. "I beg your pardon?"

"Joyce said you needed to see me tonight. What about?"

Joyce Stuck – what a low-down, dirty manipulator! I was tempted to blow the lid on the entire ruse but held back. It was too delicious. I felt like I was living in the pages of a novel. I decided to play it out.

"Well, I just didn't feel like we got a chance to finish our conversation last night. We need to talk more."

"Okay, so talk."

"Let's turn down this way." I indicated a left on Juan Diguja Street with one hand while I placed the other lightly in the small of her back to guide her. I wasn't interested in jumping right into a deep conversation, so I asked, "By the way, if you don't mind my asking, how did you get away from Dale?"

"It wasn't easy. When Joyce insisted that I see you tonight I didn't know what to do. But right after dinner I suggested to Dale that he go to bed early, since he had been traveling all last night and we have to leave early tomorrow morning for Cuenca. He said, 'I feel great, I'm not even tired,' but I kept it up until he finally agreed."

"You're a sneaky little devil, aren't you."

"Oh, please don't think that of me. I feel terrible. That is so unlike me. I've never done anything like this before."

I had obviously struck a nerve.

"Yeah, sure. Well, I'm just going to have to keep a close eye on you." I laughed.

She joined in, relieved that I was just teasing.

We walked and talked in a timeless warp. The city lights and recent rain lent a shimmering appearance to the deserted streets, like a painting by Monet. At one point, as we crossed the busy *Avenida 10 de agosto,* I offered my hand, which she took without hesitation. I savored the warm softness of it. Before long we found ourselves back on the couch of the abandoned guesthouse living room. It felt as though we had never left from the night before, or ever would need to again. Inevitably, the conversation wound its way back to my spiritual state.

"Joyce says she's sure you'll accept Christ," she began.

"Yeah, well, I think she's right."

"The thing that worries me, Kevin, is that when you get back to Tampa there won't be any Christian influence in your life."

"Well, you can set your mind at ease about that. One of the guys I share an apartment with at med school is a Christian. It's funny, I had a conversation with him just a few weeks before coming down here that was very similar to what we've talked about. I was kind of a jerk to him. I think it made him mad. Man, will he be surprised."

"I'm glad to hear about your roommate but it still scares me."

She was looking full into my face as she said it. Something stirred deep inside me. Here was someone who trusted God, yet struggled to believe that God would watch over me. Did I mean that much to her? The thought was exhilarating. On impulse I took her face in my hands and kissed her.

Chapter 30
Leslie's Surrender

I had fought the good fight. But now it was over. I still had qualms about it – after all, he hadn't actually accepted the Lord yet. But, somehow, Joyce's absolute faith and confidence that God was doing, and would continue to do, an amazing work in Kevin's life was rubbing off on me.

I surrendered myself to his embrace. All of my pent-up emotion was unleashed. I didn't just allow him to kiss me – I reveled in it. He pulled my body close to his. I abandoned my reserve to the thrill of his lips meeting mine. We stood there, kissing, wrapped in a warm embrace. The security of his arms around me sent my head spinning. He was so gentle, so tender. His strong embrace sheltered me. I felt safe and warm.

Could this really be happening to me? Could he really love me? I've never felt this way before. Sure, I'd been kissed, but never like this…

I heard the mantle clock chime four.

"This is getting to be a habit," I joked about the hours we were keeping. Reluctantly, we acknowledged that our time had come to part from one another.

"What time do you leave for Cuenca?" he asked.

"Our flight leaves at 11am, so we'll catch a taxi to the airport at 8:30."

"And what are your plans for Dale? Does he know about me?"

"No, not yet. To be honest, Joyce and I have already talked about it. Since we leave in a few hours, and you head back to Florida tomorrow, Joyce thinks

I should just wait and not say anything to Dale until he and I are on our way back to California in a couple of weeks. It will be hard, but I think she's right. There's no sense ruining his time in Ecuador."

"That's fine, but I'm not so sure I care for the idea of your traipsing all over Ecuador with some guy who wants to marry you."

I kissed him in a way that would let him know he had nothing to worry about. It wasn't until later, when I was back in my room packing for the trip, that I realized we had not made any concrete plans for seeing one another again. A cold chill came over me.

Kevin would fly back to Tampa tomorrow. What if he was playing me? Maybe this wasn't a unique experience for him like it was for me. What if he had other girls who were interested in him? I felt sick when the realization struck that there really had been no promise on his part – not even to write or call.

The more I thought and prayed about it, though, the more I had to acknowledge that God had unequivocally answered the desperate prayer I had uttered in Makuma. I couldn't deny that. I couldn't ignore it. I hoped with all my heart that this new relationship I had with Kevin would lead to marriage. But I had to admit that, even if nothing came of it, God still had shown me very clearly which path I was to take in my relationship with Dale.

A few hours later, Dale and I were on a plane headed to Cuenca. We were accompanied by Tim Drown and Dottie Walker, a veteran, single missionary serving with the Shuar. Cuenca is a beautiful, little, mountain city of white, adobe buildings crowned with red-tiled roofs. Dottie knew Cuenca well, and proved an enthusiastic guide.

She insisted we visit her favorite restaurant in the city, known for its French onion soup. My stomach was so upset from the lack of sleep and the excitement of the recent turn of events in my life. I was not at all interested in adding French onion soup to the mix. However, I didn't want to seem unappreciative toward Dottie, nor did I want to give any hint to my companions about the confusion of thoughts swirling around in my mind. When the waiter brought our soup, it was covered with a thick layer of melted, white cheese.

"What's wrong?" queried Dottie, as I sat staring at the steaming bowl.

"I'm afraid I'm not a big fan of cheese," I answered. "It's so thick," I whined.

Dottie immediately signaled the waiter and conversed back and forth with him in Spanish.

"Do you like eggs?" she asked me.

"Sure."

The waiter recovered my soup bowl and headed for the kitchen.

"He'll add some egg to dilute the cheese a bit," Dottie informed me.

Relieved, I awaited my dinner. Within moments, the waiter returned with my soup, the cheese now diluted with a raw egg floating on top! I looked aghast at the slimmey concoction. Dottie, sympathized with my predicament and dispatched the poor waiter to the kitchen once again to petition the chef to at least cook the egg for the picky patron. I appreciated all the trouble expended on my behalf but between the onion soup and my lack of sleep my stomach rebelled for the next couple days.

From Cuenca, we took a long bus ride to Dottie's home in Sucua, at the edge of the rain forest. The following day, Dale and I caught an MAF flight into Yaapi where Joyce awaited our arrival.

Joyce and Dale got along famously. Dale had brought with him the latest in fishing equipment, hammocks and back packs. He needed to evaluate their usefulness and durability and Joyce and I were only too happy to assist. Using the back packs to carry supplies on our treks through the rain forest, Joyce marveled at their comfort and practicality

I was finally able to show Dale the jungle life I loved and the people who had captured my heart.

As usual, there always seemed to be people around with nothing better to do than to watch what we were doing. I spied a little girl through the bamboo slats as she watched us.

"Look at those big eyes! Isn't she a cutie?"

Dale tried hard to respond with enthusiasm, but I could tell he was ambivalent. He seemed to enjoy fishing in the rivers but was less enamored with trudging along the muddy jungle trails. The home we stayed in was a bit too rustic for his taste. The odor of smoke and sweat that permeated the people and their dirty, ragged clothes bothered him. He had a hard time seeing past these externals to the hearts of the Shuar.

Throughout our time, Dale was very sweet. Several times he tried to hold my hand or put his arm around me to demonstrate his caring. But, for me, the thrill was gone. I was able to fend off his advances by telling him that any public display of affection was offensive in this culture. Technically, of course, that was true. But even some of the missionaries tried to be helpful by telling me that I didn't have to be **so** discrete. I was certain Dale sensed a distance between us, but neither of us chose to speak about it. That is, not until we were in the air, en route somewhere between Quito and Miami.

Leslie, pull yourself together. Don't chicken out. It's now or never.

I glanced at the man at my side. He was asleep, so I studied him. There was no denying he was good-looking. Dark, curly hair outlined a ruggedly handsome face. His large, muscular frame seemed bent on breaking free from the confines of the narrow airline seat. He was obviously no stranger to athletic pursuits.

I knew that looks weren't the most important thing. I mean, there's no doubt that it's nice to be attracted to the guy you're dating, but that shouldn't be the only, or even the major, basis of your relationship. But, in this case, that conviction only made matters worse. The truth of the matter was that he was always so thoughtful, too. I would never admit it to him, but in my heart I knew that he spoiled me.

Besides, we had so much in common. Both of us enjoyed outdoor recreation. We had spent several wonderful weekends snow skiing together at Mammoth Mountain with the College and Career group from church. As the weather warmed, he had taken me water skiing on the Colorado River. There was no doubt about it – being his girlfriend was a ton of fun.

His polite manners had scored big with my parents and that was important to me. He even enjoyed playing with my two-year old twin brothers, or at least pretended to. They were thrilled when he presented them each with a pair of boxing gloves. Most important of all, we shared the same faith. We attended the same church and most recently he seemed to be more serious about his faith. Coming to Ecuador was a big step for him. Missions were becoming something very personal to him.

So, now, why was I trying to figure out how to break up with him? I'm sure any of my friends back home would think I was crazy. I could hear them now:

"What? Leslie, do you realize what you're doing? He's a great guy and you two make a wonderful couple. Hasn't he proven his love for you over and over? What more do you want?"

From a strictly human point of view I couldn't argue with them. It's not like I had a firm offer of something better. I might be throwing away my last chance. But, the thing was, I wasn't looking at it from a strictly human point of view. I had asked the Lord, begged Him really, to show me clearly what He wanted me to do. And, for once in my life, there was no doubt that He had done that for me.

Lord, thank you for answering my prayer. Now, I need You to give me the right words to say and the courage to say them. The last thing in the world I want to do is hurt him.

In some ways I wished I had gotten this over with two weeks ago when it all happened. It would have been so much easier. But Joyce advised against it.

"No sense in ruining his time here in Ecuador," she had counseled. "Better to wait until the trip home."

At the time I recoiled at the thought of being less than open and honest. But, against my better judgment, I bowed to her wisdom. And, now that it was nearly over, I had to admit that she was right. He and I ended up having a very enjoyable time in Cuenca and Yaapi. Days spent swimming and fishing and hiking the muddy trails should have been a dream come true, and would have been, except...

Just then, his eyes fluttered and then opened, looking straight into mine.

"Oh, hi, Leslie," he said, rubbing his eyes. "I think I dozed off there for a minute."

I knew I had to go through with it. We would be landing in Miami soon. I was sure he could hear my heart

246

pounding in my chest. I summoned all my courage and resolved to go through with this. I looked him square in the face and spoke.

"Dale, there's something I need to talk to you about."

He straightened his seat back and sat upright, facing me.

"I know," he whispered. "It's just not going to work between us, is it?"

Before I could respond, he went on.

"I think I realized that during our time in the jungle, seeing how happy you were there. Our lives are moving in different directions. I can see that. I wish with all my heart it weren't so. But I want you to know how thankful I am that you came into my life when you did. I just hope I've been able to give back a fraction of the happiness you've given me."

I gulped back tears.

"Dale, I, I …"

He held a finger to my lips.

"Shhh," he said, "you don't need to say another word. Just promise me one thing?"

I nodded.

"Please don't ever change. You are one in a million, and it's been neat seeing the Lord working in you and, through you, in me. You have a unique ability to bring out the best in people. That needs to never change. Promise?"

Silent tears flowed down my cheeks.

Chapter 31
Kevin's Repentance

When I left Quito, Leslie and I still had made no arrangements for seeing one another again. But what a difference twenty-four hours can make. There was no longer any doubt in my mind that our relationship would continue and blossom.

I was looking forward to telling my roommate, Chris, all that had happened to me during those incredible three months in Ecuador. Wouldn't he be surprised at the transformation in my life? I could just picture the look on his face as I told him the story of how God had gotten the attention of his skeptical, agnostic roommate. Instead, I was the one who was in for a shock. I learned that Chris had moved in with his girlfriend in an adjacent apartment. I couldn't believe it. This was the guy who, just a few short months before, was telling me how important it was to have a right relationship with God. I was thrown into a tailspin. Did any of this God-talk mean anything? Or was it all just empty words? After struggling with it, I came to the conclusion I would need to decide how God's truth applied to me, rather than worry about how others responded to it. I needed to trust in God, not in people.

Truth didn't change in response to people's choices; nor by crossing borders. God, and my need for Him in my life, was just as real in Florida as it had been in Ecuador. I could not deny Christ's claim on my life. Alone one night in my apartment a week after my return to Tampa, I prayed to receive Christ, asking him to forgive my sins and be Lord of my life. I was at peace. I had craved a purpose in life. Now I had one, serving Him. I began building dreams of returning to Ecuador.

I was anxious to share the news of my decision with Leslie, but how? The answer came a couple of days later as I sat in my apartment reading an article from a medical journal. The article was part of the required reading for my current rotation in Child Psychiatry. Suddenly, the telephone rang.

"Hello," I mumbled, still trying to digest the obscure point of the article I was reading.

"Hi. Is this Kevin Kerrigan?" asked an unfamiliar voice.

I became wary. "Yes, it is," I said, preparing myself to rebuff the inevitable sales pitch.

"Kevin, you don't know me. I'm a ham radio operator here in Tampa. I just had a radio contact with an operator in Quito, Ecuador."

I flung the journal to the floor.

"Who was it?"

"Well, the person I talked to was a Joyce Stuck. Do you recognize that name?"

"I sure do. What did she say?"

"She asked me to pass on a message to you that another person, Leslie Williams, will be arriving in Miami on Monday, the 7th of October and staying for a week with friends. She gave me their address and phone number. Do you have a pencil and paper handy?"

I scribbled down the information, thanked the faceless messenger, and hung up the phone. My mind raced, plotting how and when I would arrive in Miami. All other thoughts were erased from my mind. The journal article remained on the floor, unread.

That week dragged on. Chris had warned me that he found the elective in Child Psychiatry rather boring. I couldn't have agreed more; and that was before

I had a compelling reason to want the time to fly by. At last, Friday afternoon arrived and I was racing south on Interstate 75 in my 1970 powder-blue Ford Maverick.

Within a few hours, I arrived at the Miami Beach address I had been given, the home of Ralph and Millie Bowen, long time friends of Leslie's parents. I learned that it was the Bowens who had arranged the blind date that introduced Leslie's folks to one another. Perhaps because of that fact, the Bowens watched us like hawks, eager to see if history was about to repeat itself. The histrionic Millie took her self-appointed role as Protector of Leslie's Virtue quite seriously. She was skeptical of me as a suitable prospect. I felt a bit uncomfortable and began to think that perhaps I had made a mistake in coming here. Leslie seemed a bit reserved and I began to wonder if her time with Dale had caused her to have second thoughts. I was dying to find out what was going on in her mind, but my curiosity was prolonged when the Bowens insisted we accompany them to the pool-side party hosted by Ralph's real estate business.

It was not until late that evening, after the Bowens had retired for the night, that Leslie and I stood alone in their kitchen. I took her in my arms and kissed her. Immediately, I knew that nothing had changed between us.

"Leslie, I want you to know that I decided to trust Christ as my savior."

"I know," she whispered.

"You do? How?"

"Oh, a little bird told me."

Not waiting for further explanation, I tightened my grip on her waist and pulled her body closer to mine. We stood kissing and talking till the wee hours of the morning.

At one point, I told her, "You know, it's amazing when I think about it. My Catholic upbringing gave me a strong sense of right and wrong, a reverence for God, and some familiarity with stories in the Bible. But I never really figured out what it was all about. Now that I understand the gospel, it's as though all the puzzle pieces I've been staring at all my life finally fit together."

"Kevin, that's wonderful, but don't let it stop there. There's so much more to learn. You just have to find some other believers to spend time with. It doesn't seem like Chris is going to be the resource you were expecting him to be. What are your plans?"

"Well, as a matter of fact, Dave Reifsnyder and his wife, Margaret, have offered to start a weekly Bible study in their home for me and any other med students that want to attend."

"Oh, Kevin, I'm so glad!"

The weekend flew by. By the end of it, we had made tentative arrangements for me to visit her family in California only two months away.

Those two months seemed to drag on forever. Our only communication came in the form of letters and occasional telephone calls. Letters were woefully inadequate to express the depth of my growing love for Leslie. Our infrequent phone conversations were kept short due to my precarious financial status as a medical student – one phone call during business hours could easily cost 40 dollars. Fortunately, other events in my life distracted me from continually focusing on time's creeping pace.

Shortly after my return from Ecuador, I changed my internship applications from pediatrics to surgery. Time was not on my side. Most of my friends had already gone for interviews at the residency programs that had extended invitations to them. I anxiously awaited word from the programs where I applied, hoping to complete the required interviews before Christmas break. One by one, I heard back from programs in Tampa, Charlottesville and Atlanta and traveled to each of those sites. In Atlanta, while interviewing at Grady Memorial Hospital, I stayed with Lou Hill in his apartment. We reminisced about the fun we had shared in Ecuador, as he showed the hundreds of slides he had taken, including the shot of the "rare, albino Amazon Indian".

My last scheduled interview was at Orange County Medical Center in California, where Leslie had worked as an intensive care nurse prior to going to Ecuador. She was no longer employed there. Instead, she had taken a job in the ICU at nearby Anaheim Memorial Hospital. My interview was scheduled for the day after I arrived in California for Christmas break. Once that was behind me, I was free to relish every second spent together with Leslie.

I loved every moment of it: meeting her family and friends, seeing where she lived and worked and where she had gone to school. Each new discovery about her strengthened my conviction that this was the woman I wanted to spend the rest of my life with.

The night after my interview at Orange County, Leslie and I stayed talking and enjoying just being together at her apartment. When I set out at 2 AM to return to her parents' house where I was to spend the night, she wrote down directions to their house as she handed me the keys to her Toyota Celica. Unfortunately, she mixed up a couple of the street names and, as a result, I lost my way. After driving all over Orange County, I pulled into a Highway Patrol station and got correct directions. By the time I dragged myself into my bedroom at her folks' house, I was exhausted and famished. There, on the bed, was a ripe, crisp apple that Leslie's mom had left for me. I was touched by her thoughtfulness.

Her parents rented a condo for a week at Mammoth Mountain. Leslie was an avid and accomplished skier. My only prior skiing experience had been on a gentle slope in the hills of Maryland. Despite my fear of heights, I threw caution to the wind, speeding downhill just barely under control, trying to keep pace with her. I was determined not to let her show me up.

One night, we sought a few moments of privacy by sitting out in front of the condo in her car. Christmas was just a few days away. I was due to fly back to Florida on the day of Christmas Eve. Most of my brothers and sisters would be home for the holidays.

"Kevin, do you really need to leave before Christmas?" she begged.

"Sorry, Leslie, but I've already got my ticket and I've told my family I would be there."

She frowned. I decided to appeal to her better instincts.

"Aren't you glad that I come from the kind of family that wants to spend the holidays together?"

"Well, yeah, I guess. But I like spending time with you too. It's just not fair," she pouted.

"At least you'll have something to remember me by," I began as I pulled a small gift-wrapped box out of my coat pocket.

She perked up.

"What? Oh, Kevin, you shouldn't have. What is it?"

"You'll just have to open it to find out."

There was a slight tremor in her hands as she removed the wrapping paper. When she saw that it was a red velvet box, the kind that usually contains jewelry, she paused and swallowed hard. Her face flushed and I thought I saw tears welling up.

All of a sudden, I realized what I had done.

Kevin, you dope. She thinks it's an engagement ring.

She opened the box to find the set of jade earrings I had chosen for her. Within seconds, she regained her composure.

"Oh, Kevin, they're beautiful. Thank you so much," as she hugged and kissed me.

Her reaction put me at ease, but still I was left with the distinct impression that she thought I was going to propose to her. There was no doubt that I was in love with her, but it just didn't seem right. After all, I had only known her for four months. I knew from previous relationships that emotions could wax and wane. It was my conviction that a man and woman should know each other for at least two years before committing to marriage. I was content to be patient and see how our relationship evolved.

That theory made perfect sense to me so long as I was together with Leslie and could enjoy the warmth of her presence. However, once I returned to Tampa and to the drudgery of written communication, I began to reconsider my position. My self-imposed two year time limit shrank in my mind to eighteen months, then twelve and, finally, six. By the time she was due to visit me in Florida in early March, I couldn't wait for the opportunity to ask her to marry me.

Then, disaster struck. On March 5th, the results of the Intern Match were made public. Each graduating medical student in the United States had ranked, in order of preference, the training programs to which he or she had applied. Those programs, meanwhile, ranked the applicants in order of their desirability. A matrix was created and on a single day of the year, each and every prospective intern knew where they would be spending the next year of their life. As the results were announced, I was elated to find that I had been accepted at my first choice – Grady Memorial Hospital in Atlanta. It was hard to imagine how life could get any better. Leslie was due to arrive in three days and we could rejoice together at the good news. However, as the exhilaration that accompanied the congratulations of my peers began to fade, self doubts began to invade my consciousness.

Grady was a very prestigious, competitive training program for surgery. How had I gotten in? When I had applied for internship at Grady, I knew I was setting my sights high. I never would have considered it had it not been for Lou Hill's encouragement.

Nothing ventured, nothing gained, I thought as I filled out the application.

But then, at the time of my interview, I regretted having had the audacity to apply to such a prestigious program. The interview was an unmitigated disaster. At one point, the interviewer, renowned plastic surgeon Dr. Maurice Jurkiewicz, had asked me what quality I felt was most important for a surgeon to possess. After fumbling around in the dark, making tentative stabs in first one direction, then another, my misery was brought to a merciful, if ignominious, end. Dr. Jurkiewicz cut through my feeble attempts to guess what answer he was looking for by stating with confidence that the answer was: integrity, as any fool would know.

Thus, my surprise at finding out that Grady had accepted me.

Was there some mistake? Had some functionary hit the wrong key on the typewriter? Were there not enough real applicants this year to fill the available positions? More to the point, was I going to be able to fake my way through an entire year of internship without being exposed for the fraud that I was?

By three days after the announcement, my self-confidence had about hit its lowest point. I had real doubts whether or not I would be able to survive the coming year, let alone take on the responsibility of another's life. It was at this precise moment that Leslie appeared on the scene, oblivious to the turmoil taking place inside of me.

Chapter 32
Leslie Betrayed

My excitement grew as our plane prepared to land in Tampa. Peering out the window, I was struck by how green everything appeared. When I had taken off from LAX earlier that day, the landscape beneath had been so brown and drab by comparison, despite the late winter rains. The lush vegetation beneath me now seemed to reflect my sense of fresh anticipation. I would soon be together with the man I loved.

Before Kevin, I had never told any man that I loved him. While still in high school I had vowed never to use the word lightly. I determined to say "I love you" only to the man I was willing to marry. I didn't ever want to use the word thoughtlessly, with no better reason than lack of having any other ready response. But that weekend in Miami, and again when he visited at Christmas, I had said those words and meant them. There was no longer any holding back.

Our courtship blossomed through letters. His visit at Christmas confirmed all my previous hopes. My parents loved him at once. I was proud to show him off to all my friends, though strangely, for the first time in my life, I really didn't care what my friends thought. There was no doubt in my mind that this was the man I wanted to spend the rest of my life with. I felt at peace that that was God's plan for me. And, though I tried to suppress the thought from my consciousness, I couldn't help but harbor the hope that, by the time I re-boarded the plane in a week, he and I would be engaged.

He was waiting for me as I burst through the gate of the jet way. Rushing to meet me, he enveloped me in an embrace and a passionate kiss. My innate self-consciousness about public displays of affection evaporated. That evening, at his apartment, our conversation turned to the future.

"I still can't believe I got accepted at Grady," he began.

"They would have been fools to let you get away. I'm just sorry that you won't be doing your internship at Orange County so we could be closer to one another and spend time together."

"We can still be together. Why don't you move to Atlanta? It's a fun city. You could get a job there and we could see each other every day."

I tried not to show my disappointment.

If he's asking me to move, he must not be sure of his love for me. He's still holding back, keeping his options open. I don't think it would be very healthy for us to be in constant contact with each other before we're married. I'm already experiencing feelings for Kevin that I've never felt for anyone before. I'm not sure I can trust myself. To move far away from family and friends might be asking for trouble. What if it didn't work out? I'm sure how I feel — he needs to be just as sure. He needs to make the next move. I already feel awkward enough flying all the way across the U. S. to visit him.

"No, I don't think so," I answered.

"But, why not?" he insisted.

"I just don't think it would be wise."

He seemed to realize my mind was made up and dropped the subject. I sensed that Kevin was wrestling with something in his mind.

He seems to really care for me; maybe he's on the verge of deciding whether or not to marry me. I don't want to be too available without any promise of a commitment on his part. If he is going to ask me to marry him, though, why is he asking me to move? I sure love being around him! I love the way he looks at me...like he's holding me with his eyes. His attentive questions and interest in every aspect of my life is just as I imagined a relationship leading to marriage should be. Well, I'll just bide my time and see what this week brings.

I couldn't wait.

The next day, after church, we drove to the house of the parents of Kevin's roommate, Chris. They owned a home on the water with a dock and a sailing boat. Kevin had made arrangements for us to go sailing with Chris and his girlfriend, Marion. Kevin seemed distracted during the twenty minute drive, almost nervous. As we pulled into the driveway at our destination, he turned to me.

"Leslie," he began, "There's something I need to tell you."

My heart began racing. I didn't say a word, allowing my body language to encourage him to continue.

"I'm not sure how to say this…"

Something in the way he said it set off an inner alarm. Thus alerted, I was still unprepared for what came next.

"I've been so mixed up lately; I'm just not sure where our relationship is going."

I couldn't believe what I was hearing. I felt nauseated.

"I mean, I know I love you, but I don't feel I love you," he concluded.

Suddenly, without warning, the world around me came to a standstill. Wave after wave of emotion rolled over me – shock, anger, betrayal, hopelessness. I just sat there, stunned. The shameful truth was, I knew exactly how he felt, or thought I did.

While still in college, I had dated a seminary student named Leighton. He was a wonderful, Godly man of integrity. I respected him greatly and enjoyed spending time with him. Apparently, for him, the feelings went deeper than respect. One evening, after a fun day of skiing, he asked me to marry him. It caught me off guard. I knew he cared for me, but I really didn't expect a marriage proposal. After all, our relationship was not exclusive. I never tried to hide the fact that I continued to date others, besides him. When he proposed, my heart was in turmoil.

I liked Leighton very much and really respected him; and I knew that respect was a good foundation for marriage. He had proven himself a good friend and had been my confidant through some difficult times of questioning my faith during college. But the truth was, there was no, or at least not much, spark or excitement at being with him. There had been plenty of opportunity to grow to love him and I hoped I would. We had counseled together at camps and I helped him at a conference he led. He was a dynamic speaker and leader. I admired him greatly, but I just didn't feel anything more than a deep friendship for him. Finally, after weeks of struggling with his proposal, I had to tell him "no".

Now I could see that Kevin regarded me in the same way. I understood all too well what he was saying. He admired me for the person I was, but felt no spark, no emotion, and no chemistry. I was devastated.

Leslie, you have made a complete fool of yourself. Oh, Lord, what am I doing here?

Just then, Chris and Marion came up to the car to greet us. Marion was a beautiful girl and I couldn't help but compare myself to her.

No wonder Kevin has no feelings for me. Look at the competition.

Soon we were slicing through the green waters of Tampa Bay beneath a cloudless sky. It should have been a romantic dream-come-true. Instead, I sought to hide my hurt alone on the foredeck. Kevin spoke to me a few times, but I felt he was just trying to be polite.

He must really be ashamed to be with me – this square, homely girl from California who chased him all the way across the country. How embarrassing!

My fears that he was embarrassed to be seen with me were confirmed that evening when he suggested we go to the movies to see Agatha Christie's *Murder on the Orient Express.* He hardly said two words to me. I felt as though he wished I had never come to Tampa.

The following morning was Monday, and Kevin had to return to his Neurology rotation at the VA hospital. I was left alone in my hurt and disappointment. I decided to call my mom. I wanted to fly back to California early, but didn't know how I could change my ticket. As always, she offered encouragement and wise counsel.

"Oh, Les, I am so sorry. I know you must be feeling very hurt. But I can't believe that this is the end of it all. Kevin has certainly given every indication that he really cares for you."

I couldn't control my sobbing.

"Why don't you just stick it out and make the best of it?" continued Mom. "You've already taken the time off work. Just treat him as a friend and see what comes of it."

I knew she was right. My mom always helped me to see things more clearly. Kevin needed a Christian friend. I was still concerned about him and his relationship with Christ. If the Lord had brought us together for no other purpose than for me to encourage him in his Christian walk, I was willing to fulfill that role.

"Thanks, Mom. It helps to hear you say it."

I resolved to follow my mother's advice.

Even if nothing works out between us, at least Kevin knows the Lord now. I really care about him and want the best for him. I'll make the most of my remaining time in Florida.

Once I resolved it in my mind that way, it was easier to be myself and enjoy Kevin's company. He responded by seeming much more relaxed and attentive toward me. The rest of the week in Tampa was fun and by Friday we were ready to go to Orlando to meet Kevin's parents. Kevin got off work early that day and decided we should stop en route to Orlando at Hillsborough River State Park, just east of Tampa.

It was a lovely, sunny day and we decided to canoe on the lazy river. Kevin steered the canoe from his seat in the stern in and out among the low, overhanging branches of live oak. Soon, we were completely alone, except for the many small alligators sunning themselves on half-submerged logs. The muffled silence of the still, humid air was broken only by the crescendo hum of cicadas, hidden along the banks.

"This is so much fun," I said. "There's nothing like this in California, since we don't really have any rivers. About the closest we have is the jungle ride at Disneyland. You know, the one where the guide shoots a hippopotamus that comes up right in front of the boat. Do you know what I'm talking about? Have you been on that?"

Silence.

"You know. They probably have it here in Florida at Disney World, too. Don't they?"

There was still no answer, so I turned around, only to find the back of the canoe empty! I began to imagine Kevin underwater, wrestling with an alligator, until my eyes were drawn upriver to a figure dangling from a low-hanging branch we had earlier passed beneath. Kevin had reached up, grabbed the branch and pulled himself from the canoe without making a sound. When he saw that I had spotted him, he began shouting.

"Help! Get back up here, quick. I don't know how much longer I can hold on."

I couldn't believe Kevin! I burst out laughing at sight of him dangling from the overhanging branch. I was laughing so hard I could hardly maneuver the canoe to a point beneath him. I toyed with the idea of letting him fall into the river for having played that trick on me, but I decided against it when I saw the alligators dropping from their sunny perches to the water below. Besides, he was so much fun, and full of surprises. I felt my heart being drawn to him once again.

We continued our journey to Orlando, singing along with tapes of Simon & Garfunkel as we drove. I worked up my nerve and scooted across the front seat to sit next to him. I studied him as we traveled. Judging from the way he was treating me it sure seemed as though he liked me. I loved his humble attitude. There was no doubt in my mind that he was smart – much smarter than me – yet he never flaunted his intelligence. When he had been around my friends he took an interest in others, asked questions of them. He seemed to be very comfortable with himself and with others and always treated people with respect regardless of their position in life – from little children to the gardener at his apartment complex. It made me proud to be with him. It seemed so natural to be together. But one nagging thought kept inserting itself, despite my best efforts to ignore it.

What if we were only going to continue as friends? Do I really want to let my heart get drawn into a bond that might get broken? Shouldn't I hold back?

As we drove up to Kevin's parents' home, I was impressed by the large, white pillars spanning the front of the house. It was obvious that they had done well financially, despite having raised seven children. But I knew, too, that their success in life was more than just financial. Their nearly thirty years of marriage served as an example of stability, commitment and love to Kevin and his siblings. He had told me that he really admired his parents' relationship. He could remember seeing them, not long before, walking together on the beach holding hands like young lovers. I knew his family was very important to Kevin. He had proven that to me when he left California on the day before Christmas so that he could spend Christmas with his family. I was glad that family mattered to Kevin, but it made it sort of intimidating to meet his folks.

What will they be like? I wonder if they'll like me. I enjoy meeting new people, so why am I feeling so nervous?

Their warm welcome and natural interest in me put me at ease very quickly.

But, though we continued to enjoy each other's company the remainder of my visit, by the time I boarded the plane for my return trip to California, there was still no promise of a future together, nor even an indication of where our relationship was headed. Rather than a ring on my finger, I boarded the plane wearing heavy doubts that weighed me down.

The way he kissed me and held me when we parted makes me think he really is interested in me. But he didn't **say** *anything – not "I'll write" or "I'll call" – nothing about our future; not a word. It seems like we're together emotionally, but I don't know. I may be wrong about everything. I need to start thinking about my future and begin making plans. Maybe I need to investigate opportunities on the mission field. There's really nothing holding me back now. I've passed my boards and gotten a couple of years of nursing experience. Maybe it's time to start heading in that direction.*

Chapter 33
Kevin's Recovery

By the time we parted, I was convinced beyond a shadow of a doubt that this was the woman for me. The way she responded in the week following my asinine statement of "I know I love you, but I don't feel I love you," confounded and amazed me. I had broken off relationships with girls before, so I knew what to expect: anger, hurt, blame and an unspoken desire to get even. But, after recovering from the initial shock, Leslie showed none of that. Instead of trying to protect herself, she continued to look out for me. Her unexpected response caused me to wake up and realize how much I loved this remarkable woman. It also made me embarrassed for the unnecessary pain I had put her through.

Okay, now what, Genius? You can't just say, "I was only kidding when I told you 'I know I love you, but I don't feel I love you'. She'll think you're a complete idiot and that your words mean nothing. No, it will be better to not say anything and just show her how much she means to you.

With that unassailable plan firmly in mind, I was buoyant with anticipation as I returned from Tampa International Airport after seeing her off. I immediately began plotting to purchase a ring in anticipation of asking for her hand in marriage.

About that time, I got an unexpected phone call. It was Wally Swanson! He and his family had just returned from Ecuador on furlough. They were en route, driving from mission headquarters near Miami to their home turf in Minneapolis and wondered if they could stop by Tampa for a visit. We got together that weekend for a picnic lunch in a nearby park. It was so good to see them again. It brought back so many pleasant memories.

We rejoiced together about my having committed my life to the Lord. They had already heard about that through the grapevine. But, being assured of the reality of that relationship, there was another relationship that they were anxious to find out about. As usual, Charlotte wasted no time in getting down to brass tacks.

"So, what's happening with you and Leslie?"

"Well, as a matter of fact," I responded, deciding it best not to mention anything about my boneheaded *faux pas*, "I've decided to marry her!"

I suppose it was a bit presumptuous of me to put it that way. I mean, Leslie did have the option of refusing my offer of marriage. But I would not have wanted to change anything that had already happened even if she did refuse. My life was changed forever with or without Leslie by my side. But, somehow, I felt that God would not have brought us as far as He had without seeing it through to the end.

Charlotte beamed her approval as tears welled in her eyes.

"That's wonderful, Kevin," Wally said. "You know, it's really unique the way the Lord brought you two together. You'll always have that to look back on when you hit rough times in your marriage."

After they left, and for the next several days, I pondered what Wally meant by hitting "rough times". After all, I was about to marry the perfect girl.

Oh well, I'll think about that more later on.

In the meantime, I increased the frequency, length and intensity of the letters that I wrote to Leslie, convinced that this would show her the depth of my feeling for her. I also began calling her almost daily, despite the disappointment of continually finding her not at home.

Secure in the knowledge that she couldn't help but respond to so urgent a display of true affection, I couldn't wait to hear back from her. Finally, after quite some time, a letter from her appeared in my mailbox. Well, not exactly a letter –a postcard! It read:

> Kevin,
>   Thanks for the great time I had with you and your family.
>   I really enjoyed myself.
>   Leslie

That was it! No "Dear Kevin", no "Love, Leslie". Nothing. I could almost feel the ice dripping off of the card.

Desperate with fear that I was about to lose the woman of my dreams, I redoubled my efforts to convince her of my ardent, unchangeable love for her.

Chapter 34
Making Plans

I made sure I was very busy when I returned from Florida. I began praying seriously about where the Lord would have me serve. In my heart, I still held out hope that Kevin had feelings for me, but I didn't want to rely on that possibility.

There was nothing standing in the way of my applying with a mission organization. I had heard about a hospital ship that went to places and cared for needy people, doing surgeries and holding clinics. That sounded like a wonderful thing to be involved in. On the other hand, I could always go back to Ecuador and work in one of their hospitals. I started looking into some possibilities. I had nearly two years of nursing experience. Now was a perfect time. But where should I serve?

I had pictured myself serving in the Congo ever since I heard about the need from the missionary speaker at church who had inspired me to study nursing in the first place. But I heard about changes going on in that country, recently re-named Zaire, which were making it more difficult for missionaries to enter. Should I consider returning to Ecuador? It would be nice to go to someplace that was familiar.

I also began dating other guys again. I had always enjoyed the company of men. If things with Kevin weren't going to work out, then I needed to keep my options open. Besides, it was a good way to get my mind off of him. However, it didn't have quite the effect I had hoped. I found that when I did go out, I was made painfully aware of how the other men fell far short of what I saw in Kevin. I felt like there was a big hole in my heart. But, I wanted to serve the Lord, and I couldn't wait around to see what Kevin was going to do. As I prayed and considered my options I started to get excited about going to the mission field.

About this time, I began receiving letters almost daily from Kevin. He was opening up and sharing details of his life – little frustrations and successes of his current rotation in Pulmonary Medicine; insights he had gained at church or in the Reifsnyder's Bible study; plans for moving to Atlanta to start his internship. I felt like each revelation opened up a little window into his heart. Everything I learned made me admire and respect him that much more. Before long, I realized my heart was being drawn back to him, despite my half-hearted attempts to protect it. One day he called while I was home.

"Leslie! How great to hear your voice. You're a hard person to get a hold of."

"Yeah, I know. I've been busy. Work has been very demanding."

"Well, that's okay. It doesn't matter, now that I've finally gotten you. I want to hear all about what you've been up to. But, first, I need to ask you something. I've been thinking. I've got two weeks between graduation and the start of internship. What would you think of me coming out there for a visit?"

"Oh, that would be great!"

My heart raced.

*So, maybe he **is** interested in me…maybe more than a friend. What would this visit be like?….what does this mean?*

I continued working and looking into mission opportunities. My old roommate Ruth was looking into a short term mission to China. I had never had an interest in China but her decision made me feel that I needed to make a decision…soon. I just couldn't quite get myself to move towards an actual commitment. I was dragging my feet.

June came and I headed to Los Angeles County Airport to pick up Kevin. He had taken a "red eye special" in order to save money, so his plane arrived in the early hours of the morning. I searched for his face in the crowd coming out of the gangway. When I saw him our eyes met and soon we were locked in an embrace. His kiss did not seem like one of friendship. I could have stayed there forever. By the time we arrived back at my apartment it was 5 AM. The lack of sleep didn't keep us from talking. It was one of the things I loved about our time together – we never seemed to run out of conversation. It all seemed so natural, at least at first. As our conversation continued, Kevin grew distracted, then almost agitated. It brought back memories of our conversation in the driveway of Chris' parents' house. I began to brace myself for the worst.

But then, just as my anxiety level was rising, he dropped to a knee and produced a little ring-sized box. I looked into his eyes…

Was this some kind of a cruel joke?

"Leslie, I love you," he said. "Will you marry me?"

I opened the box. This time it was actually a gold ring with a beautiful solitary diamond!

Was this really happening to me?

I could contain my excitement no longer and threw my arms around his neck.

"Yes, I would love to marry you! I'd be very proud to be your wife."

My eyes filled with tears of joy as we hugged and kissed. I put the ring on my finger. It fit perfectly!

"How did you know what size to make it?"

"Ruth took one of your other rings and got it sized for me. I asked her to do that for me one of the times I called you when you were out."

"You little sneak!" I smiled.

"So, how does a June wedding sound to you?" he asked.

"You mean next June?" My smile disappeared and my shoulders sagged. "Why not in December?"

"Okay, then," he countered, "how about November?"

We rushed home to my parents' house to give them the wonderful news. They were overjoyed. They knew how much I loved Kevin and were reassured by this turn of events. Kevin had already told his folks of his plans to ask me to marry him.

"What did they say?" I was anxious to know their response.

"They were very pleased. My mom told me that my previous fiancée was fine as a girlfriend, but that you're the kind of girl I should marry."

Now that both sets of parents knew, we were anxious to share our secret with the woman who had played such a big part in choreographing our romance. Joyce was home in southern California on furlough. We rushed over to the mission house on West Maple Street in Orange, where she and the kids were staying. As we pulled up in front of the home, Joyce and the kids ran up to greet us. Having recently arrived, they were in the process of re-arranging the furniture and setting up the home for their six month stay. We pitched in to help. Joyce was so pre-occupied with the project that she failed to notice the stunning object on my left hand, despite my blatant attempts to get her attention. Finally, I stopped working and just waved my hand in front of her face. Her face lit up as she began shouting.

"What!" she shouted. "You're engaged? Is it true? That's wonderful. You're getting married! Oh, but when will the wedding be? Will I still be here?"

"Well, you better be. How could we get married without you there? I was hoping you would do the guest book."

"I'd be honored!" she beamed.

All of us hugged and laughed and shared memories of our time together in Kapawari and Quito. It had all seemed so far away, but now the memories and emotions they carried came rushing back.

Chapter 35

And the two shall become one flesh

In a burst of activity, all the arrangements for the wedding were made. Then came the hard part – waiting. At last November came and along with it all the guests arrived. At the rehearsal dinner, our fathers made a remarkable discovery. Since both of them were retired Marine Corps officers, they naturally began comparing notes about acquaintances they had in common and duty stations where they had served. During the course of their conversation, they discovered that, twenty-two years earlier, they had both been stationed at the Marine Corps base in Quantico, Virginia. Both families had lived in the military housing at Thomason Park in adjacent apartment buildings. We were neighbors as three-year-olds and may well have played together in the sandbox!

The next day, November 22, 1975, dawned bright and clear. The California smog lifted to reveal the nearby mountains. That day, we became man and wife at the beautiful, little, stone chapel at Fairhaven Cemetery. We were so happy, we couldn't stop smiling. Even losing Kevin's ring before the ceremony was not enough to dampen Leslie's spirits. God had in no uncertain terms answered the desperate cry of a young woman's heart and had revealed Himself to a young man wanting to believe, but afraid of the consequences.

Wedding Day

The first years of our marriage went by like a blur. While Kevin was buried under the demands of internship and residency training, Leslie was not idle.

And the two shall become one flesh

She delivered our fifth son before we celebrated our seventh anniversary!

Shortly after the birth of our first son, Kevin penned the following lines:

Lord, give me the words that I need to express
The longing and loving and deep tenderness
That fills me and thrills me when toward her my thoughts
Turn, revealing the wonders through her that you've wrought.

She found me a sinner apart from you, Lord
Then slowly with patience, with prayer and with words
She showed me that you are the center, not I;
That in order to live fully, first I must die.

She found me when I thought my love had been spent
But until there was her, I knew not what love meant;
Cautiously, carefully she entered my life
Until – blessing of blessings! – we became man and wife.

And just when I thought that her giving was done
She responded by giving more – and bore me a son.
Now each dawn I awaken I'm anxious to see
What new grace You've directed through her unto me.

We are well aware that our story is not typical. Many would look askance at the risks we were taking in marrying. In moments of lucid reasoning, we would have to agree with them. But then our hearts remind us of what would have been lost by ignoring the clear prompting of God. He showed us in no uncertain terms that He is Lord and will not be contained by man's limited imagination. In the end, we know this is not our story, but His. True, Leslie's heart was searching and Kevin's mind was testing during those fateful days in Kapawari and Quito. But, in a larger sense, it was God who was doing the searching and testing. Jeremiah 17:10 says: "I, the Lord, search the heart, I test the mind." *Searching Heart, Testing Mind.* Ours are the adjectives. God is the verb.

Epilogue

On October 25, 1974, a month after our eventful week in Quito, Joyce had written a letter to coworkers who were on furlough in the U. S. In part, it read:

> *To make a long story short, there's real interest between Leslie and Kevin. In fact, I'm sure that eventually they will marry and be back here as missionaries.*

We did. Following Kevin's surgical training and military service, we returned to Ecuador with our family. We arrived back in time to celebrate our tenth anniversary at the Hotel Quito. On our fifteenth anniversary we flew out to Kapawari.

By the time we had returned to Shell, the new *Hospital Vozandes del Oriente* had been built across the Motolo River from the old site. We helped others transform the old hospital into a guest house for the many visitors to Shell. We lived in the old Fuller house and later in the Swanson house. Our sons attended Nate Saint Memorial School, the little mission school begun by Charlotte Swanson. They jumped off the Alpayacu Bridge and challenged visitors to do the same.

From time to time, we would stop at the old hospital kitchen and relive the moment when it all began. In the space of a few short months, God had given Kevin a new direction for his career, a new life in Him and a woman with whom to share the rest of his days on earth. In that same time, He had shown Himself faithful to a young woman willing to trust Him with her future.

And what of the others who played such crucial roles in that epochal time of our lives? Sara Risser continued to serve in Ecuador in a variety of roles, including managing a Christian camp for disabled children and starting a ministry for families of prison inmates. Doug Peters eventually became Assistant to the President of HCJB. He and Darlene served with HCJB for thirty-nine years. Dr. Wally Swanson retired to his beloved Ecuador after thirty-two years of caring for the poorest of that country's sick and injured. Char Swanson began a popular Bible study, *Camino de la Luz*, which is still being taught in Quito following her death from ovarian cancer in 2002.

Following several near-misses, pilot Dave Osterhus transferred from MAF to GMU, where he and wife Carol continue to serve in the U. S. as area representatives for the Midwest. Their son, Dan, returned to Shell as an MAF pilot. There he met and married Sue Thomas, a teacher at Nate Saint Memorial School. Dan died in a flying accident while searching for a downed plane near Shell in 1997. Sue and their baby, Phoebe, returned to Shell following Dan's death.

The Ecuadorian nurse, Irene Molina de Velastegui, who was learning to administer anesthesia that summer, served as Nursing Director at the Shell hospital for many years. We were honored to attend her retirement ceremony in 2003 on one of our many return visits to Ecuador.

Chiki is now a health promoter in her village of Yuvientsa. Her husband, Chuvi, is a leader of the Shuar indigenous church. They have ten children.

Leslie's roommate, Ruth, and her husband, Scott Hall, served as missionaries in Hong Kong.

Joyce Stuck served as GMU's dorm mom in Quito, and then spent several years back in California while her kids attended college. Shortly after we returned to Shell, Joyce joined us at Hospital Vozandes Oriente. There she used her language skills and background as an LVN to function as a nurse/social worker/chaplain for the many Shuar patients. It was amazing to see. Stoic and somber Shuar patients would view with suspicion this large *gringa* approaching them. But the minute she opened her mouth, their faces would light up. It wasn't just that she knew their language. She knew **them** – their culture, the places they lived, often their friends and relatives. No matter the circumstances, she always exuded joy and the quiet confidence that a loving God was in control. And she always gave them a reason to hope, just as she had done for us many years before.

1418919

Made in the USA